THE BASICS OF
RC HELIS

MODEL
Airplane
NEWS

CONTENTS

Published by Air Age Media Inc.
20 Westport Road, Wilton CT 06897
On the web at: airage.com

PRINTED IN THE USA

AirAGE
MEDIA

This book will help you through the learning stages of flying radio control helicopters—and into aerobatics—with minimum hardship to you and your helicopter. I will take you through this learning process not with formulas or theory but with everyday common sense and practical knowledge, so you'll progress from just thinking of getting into RC helicopters to being a successful chopper pilot.

The information presented covers strictly the procedures and techniques I use in selecting, building and flying a model helicopter. These I have learned from experience, both good and bad, and from watching and talking to others as they fly. There is no reason why everyone needs to suffer the learning process many of us did years ago when there was no one to help, and there was very little material to read on the subject. Many have tried to teach themselves to fly helicopters without any outside help, but the probability of success was rather low. After a few mishaps, many gave it up as being too hard and too costly when, in reality, it isn't either.

THE THREE QUESTIONS

Three of the questions I'm most often asked are:
1. How hard are helicopters to fly?
2. How much does it cost to get started?
3. Is it better to fly airplanes first? Since these questions arise so often, they may also have occurred to you.

First, how hard are helicopters to fly? Think back to when you learned how to ride a bicycle. I can remember trying to ride, only to fall down, dust myself off and try again. After a while, I felt as if I would never be able to do it, even though all the other guys could. That discouragement didn't last too long, though, and soon I tried

again. And, as we all know, success came rather quickly. This little story actually has a lot of similarities with learning to fly a helicopter because in the beginning, you have virtually no control of the helicopter and don't think you ever will have. Then, one day, you'll be able to hover—not for very long or very high, but it will be a hover, and you'll almost feel a little control over the machine that couldn't be controlled. The other amazing thing about helicopters is that once you learn how to hover and fly around, you never forget—just like riding a bike. I haven't ridden a bike in some time, but I know I still can, and it's the same with helicopters. I hope to make this learning process as quick and as crash-free as possible for you.

The second question—how much will it cost to get into the hobby?—is harder to answer because it depends on the quality and size of helicopter, radio, etc., you choose. But even moderately priced helicopters fly very well, and that wasn't always true. I cover some specific options for a helicopter, radio, etc., in the first few

chapters to make you more knowledgeable about choosing your equipment. I think you should get the best equipment you can comfortably afford because better equipment is a good long-term investment. If you really like helicopters, as I think you will, your initial investment in better equipment will pay dividends for a long time. Even if you choose the less expensive equipment, plan to spend at least $500 to get started, but you could reduce that sum by purchasing good used equipment.

And your family may join you in your new hobby, so your monetary investment may pay big family dividends in the form of enjoyment for the whole family. And isn't that what you're looking for in a hobby?—enjoyment and someone to share it with.

The last question—is it better to start with RC airplanes?—is difficult to answer with any certainty. Any experience flying RC planes will be helpful, but you don't need to fly airplanes before you try helicopters.

First you must learn how to hover, either with the help of a flight simulator or your own helicopter. In either case, your practicing should be at no more than 1 or 2 feet off the ground. If you can hover at 1 foot, you can hover at 100 feet, but keeping close to the ground while you practice minimizes the risk to your helicopter. If you don't fly RC airplanes, there are several advantages to starting with helicopters: you don't need a flying field or a runway; improvements in mufflers reduce engine noise, so you can practice in any open field or even your backyard; and because an instructor isn't needed for takeoffs and landings, you can practice whenever you have the time.

WHAT TO EXPECT

I assume you have virtually no experience with model helicopters or airplanes, so any experience you do have will be a benefit that will help you to progress faster.

The first few chapters concentrate on the helicopter and its related equipment; the different types of equipment available; their good and bad points; the limitations you will have to live with, etc. If you have already purchased a helicopter, you may wish to jump ahead to the chapters that are of more immediate interest to you, such as those on building, making initial adjustments, etc. In any case, we'll go through building and setup and then on to hovering; then we'll transition to forward flight and finish with aerobatics and advanced maneuvering. Initially, you will use the techniques I give you, but as you progress, you will develop techniques to suit your equipment, type of flying, weather conditions, etc. It's important to remember that there is no right or wrong way to fly, so experiment and use the techniques that suit you best.

Learning to be a good helicopter pilot takes a lot of practice, concentration and patience, so don't

get discouraged if you don't progress as fast as you would like. We all went through the same learning process, and with determination and practice, you'll look back and wonder why it seemed hard in the beginning.

SAFETY

Safety must be foremost throughout our building and flying. Because of its large spinning rotors, a helicopter is potentially the most dangerous of all RC models. Proper construction is vital to safety. A poorly constructed helicopter will almost invariably malfunction, and that could cause you to lose control and crash. I certainly don't need to elaborate on the dangers of having an out-of-control helicopter. Therefore, build the helicopter according to its manufacturer's instructions, run preflight checks before every flight, never fly too close to yourself or spectators, and follow the safe flying techniques I present.

ASK FOR HELP

Never be too proud or too shy to ask for advice or help from those who have more experience. This is especially important before you first try hovering. I hope this book will answer just about all your questions, but I'm sure I don't cover every one, and the answers to a few questions will make all the difference to your progress.

Not only should you ask questions, but you should also have someone with more experience check your helicopter as you build it. A more experienced eye can pick out even minor mistakes before they become big ones.

NOMENCLATURE

You'll notice that I refer to the controls of a helicopter as if they were on an airplane. I'll refer to right cyclic as right aileron, the tail rotor as rudder, etc. This should reduce confusion because if I said I was

applying right tail rotor, some readers would think I want the tail to go to the right and others would think I want the nose to go the right. But if I say we are applying right rudder, that means we are applying a right-rudder command through the transmitter to make the nose go to the right. Similarly, right aileron means to move the control stick to the right to produce right cyclic to make the helicopter bank to the right, etc.

EQUIPMENT RECOMMENDATIONS

I mention and show several helicopters, radios, types of support equipment, etc., but I'm not writing product reviews or recommending any particular products. My purpose is to inform, so I have asked manufacturers and distributors to send me samples of their equipment so that I may give you an idea of what is available and show you how to use it properly. I'm grateful to the companies that responded, and I've listed them at the end of this book.

ACADEMY OF MODEL AERONAUTICS (AMA)

The AMA is an organization for those who are interested in model aviation, and it has been in existence for more years than I care to remember. It represents us in Congress and to other government agencies to ensure that our interests in radio-control frequency allocation and flying-site preservation are well heard so that we can continue our country's modeling heritage. In addition, the AMA provides insurance for our flying fields, for spectators who watch us fly and for us when we fly. If you are not a current AMA member, consider joining now. Either see you local hobby shop for more information on the AMA and an application, or visit the association's website at www.modelaircraft.org.

After 23 years of flying fighters for the U.S. Air Force and 13 years as an airline pilot for US Airways, Paul Tradelius is now retired and regularly flies model helicopters. His long professional flying career included flying combat in Vietnam, being a military instructor pilot, a flight examiner and a test pilot for the F-16. He would never have enjoyed such a long career as a pilot had he not discovered model airplanes at an early age and been encouraged by his loving and devoted mother, who ensured that he received an education.

Paul's interest in modeling began with rubber-powered models, and when he was seven, he was given his first .049 engine-powered airplane. From then on, he knew that airplanes would feature prominently in his life, and he read books on aircraft design and mathematics with a view to one day designing and building his own planes. At the age of 15, he was given his first radio control set—a monster with tubes and batteries that had to be tuned before every flight. Even so, he felt lucky to have some control of his plane, albeit limited.

He attended the University of Oklahoma, where he earned a bachelor of science degree in Aeronautical and Space Engineering. Following his graduation, he was commissioned a second lieutenant in the U.S. Air Force and entered its jet-pilot training course. Later, he earned a master's degree in Engineering Management from Southern Methodist University.

Throughout his Air Force career, he continued to fly RC airplanes, and in 1981, while stationed in Germany flying the F-4 Phantom, he decided to give the new RC helicopters a try. At that time, very few people flew RC helicopters, and there was very little to read about them. He had to learn everything on his own, so he crashed a lot. Paul therefore enjoys writing to help others so that they won't have to go through a comparably difficult learning process.

He now enjoys all types of helicopter flying, including scale and aerobatics, and he continues to experiment with modifications to improve his helicopters' performance.

He hopes this book will help you as you progress with your flying of RC helicopters. Because our hobby is ever expanding and changing, it's impossible for any one person to know it all, so please use this book as a starting point.

FLIGHT SIMULATORS

Flight Simulators

Although model helicopters have been flying since the mid-1970s, only since the early 1990s have simulators been available to help us to learn to fly. For those of you who are too young to remember what computers were like in that era, the personal computer (PC) was very limited in its speed, capacity and ease of use. This means that the first helicopter simulators were slow, had poor graphics and did not accurately simulate the handling of a model helicopter—at least, by today's standards.

Since then, computers and simulators have progressed to a point at which the simulator does an excellent job of representing the helicopter in a very lifelike manner, and increased processing speeds provide a virtually instantaneous response to our control inputs. But to get the maximum benefit from any simulator, the computer must meet the simulator's requirements for processing speed, hard-drive capacity, video card, etc.

As I mentioned in the introduction, flying a helicopter is much like riding a bike. Someone can tell you how to ride a bike until they are blue in the face, but it does no good at all until you get on a bike and get a feel for the balance and control for yourself. Flying helicopters is much the same. You have to develop a feel for the balance and control that are unlike anything you have ever experienced before. Then, add the difficulty

Figure 1-1. The *Reflex XTR* is available for use only with your transmitter. It has the best video presentation I have seen; I could discern individual blades of grass, powerlines, etc. In English, German and French, it has a unique training feature described in the instructions, and it allows the extensive modification of model parameters to customize flight characteristics.

of flying the helicopter while you're on the ground. We are so used to being inside a car, for instance, that we're used to seeing and feeling the needed control inputs. But all our flying is outside and away from the helicopter—sometimes at great distances.

A computer simulator offers many benefits both to novices who want to hover and do autorotations and to advanced fliers who are interested in practicing advanced 3D maneuvers.

These benefits include:

Fly before you buy. If you are not sure that a model helicopter is really right for you, try a simulation first. Many simulators come

with their own controller (transmitter) that will let you get the feel of flying before you invest in an actual RC helicopter, engine, radio, etc.

Fly in any weather at any time. You don't have to wait for the weekend or a nice day to practice your latest maneuver.

Change the weather. Change the direction and speed of the wind, add turbulence and alter other flight parameters to make your training more realistic.

No fear of crashing. All learning mistakes on the computer are immediately repairable at no cost, so you can fly with reckless abandon.

Save the cost of fuel. This is especially important if you fly the larger, .90 helicopters that use 12 to 16 ounces of fuel for each flight.

No wear and tear on your helicopter, radio, etc. Although helicopters and their associated equipment last a long time by any standards, flying time on the simulator is virtually unlimited.

Fly a variety of models at different airfields. Most simulators have a list of helicopters and airplanes and a variety of flying sites to choose from, all of which make the learning fun.

Simulate your own helicopter. You can alter the model's parameters to closely resemble the performance of your own helicopter.

Vary helicopter parameters. Pitch curves, throttle curves, swashplate efficiency, etc., can be altered, so you can experiment with changes you might want to make to your RC helicopter.

Figure 1-2. The Dave Brown Products *Radio Control Flight Simulator 2001* can be used only with the included controller. As far as I know, it's the smallest controller on the market, and this can be an advantage for younger people with smaller hands. It also uses a gameport interface connector that is compatible with older computers, but a gameport-to-USB adapter is available to use with any computer.

Safe areas keep you out of no-fly zones. Some simulators warn you if you fly too close to yourself, the pits, etc. This makes your training very close to what it will be like at your local flying field.

System failures test and improve your flying skills. You can program in the possibility of having an engine or radio failure at an unexpected time during flight to see how you would handle such an emergency.

Built-in training system. Some programs will allow you to control only part of the helicopter, and the simulator controls the rest. For example, you can choose to control only the aileron function and leave all the other control functions to the simulator. Once you feel comfortable with your performance, you can add other control functions.

Website updates. As simulator programs improve and new helicopters are added, the updates are available online from the simulation's website. Simulator add-ons are also available on CDs to expand the capabilities of your simulator with new helicopters, airplanes and flying sites.

Practice with your own radio. Many simulators allow you to connect your helicopter transmitter to your computer. This allows you to get the feel of your own

Figure 1-3. The Great Planes *RealFlight R/C Flight Simulator G-3* can be used with the company's full-function controller or with your transmitter. It can create and edit airports, induce flight failures and participate in events such as pylon racing, limbo flying and spot landings. "Add-on" volumes are available to expand its already tremendous capabilities.

Figure 1-4. The *Aerofly Professional Deluxe* from Ikarus can be used with Aerofly's controller or your transmitter. It features several flying sites in Germany, can be used by one or two players and played in English, German, or French. It also has a website that supplies information updates, free downloads and customer support.

position" as described in the beginning of chapter 15.

There are a variety of ways to hold the transmitter sticks. For precise, smooth control inputs, I find it best to place my thumb on top of the control stick and then place the meaty part of my index finger (the part between the tip of the finger and the first joint) on the front of the control stick. Then I slide my index finger up the front of the control stick until it just touches the base of my thumb. The thumb completely controls the helicopter throughout the entire stick range, while the index finger steadies and improves the accuracy of your control movements—much as leaning against a tree steadies someone with a rifle prior to firing.

Although simulators have many benefits, it's important to remember that they only simulate. No matter how good a simulation might be, there is nothing like hovering your own helicopter with its unique characteristics, engine sound, exhaust smell and your own sense of anxiety! So if you enjoy flying your simulator, you'll really love flying your own helicopter.

control sticks, operate the transmitter switches, use a transmitter tray, etc., just as you will use them at the flying field. However, because the transmitter antenna will not be extended while you're at your computer, unplug the transmitter module, or frequency crystal, to avoid damaging the output transistor. This will also reduce the transmitter battery load and extend the training time between charges.

Not all simulators have all these features, and improvements are ongoing, so choose the simulator that has the features that are most important to you. Refer to the "Source Guide" later in this book for the websites of the featured simulators to get their updated capabilities and computer-system requirements.

When you use any simulator, train in the way you intend to fly at the flying field, and then fly in the way you trained at home. Use your own transmitter whenever

you can; use a neck strap or a transmitter tray to support the transmitter; hold the control sticks in a comfortable and proper manner; use the required switches and internal transmitter computer functions just as you will to adjust your own helicopter; and keep the helicopter in the "standard hover

Figure 1-5. Thumbs on top of control sticks with index fingers in front for support allows a full range of movement with positive, precise control.

SELECTING A HELICOPTER

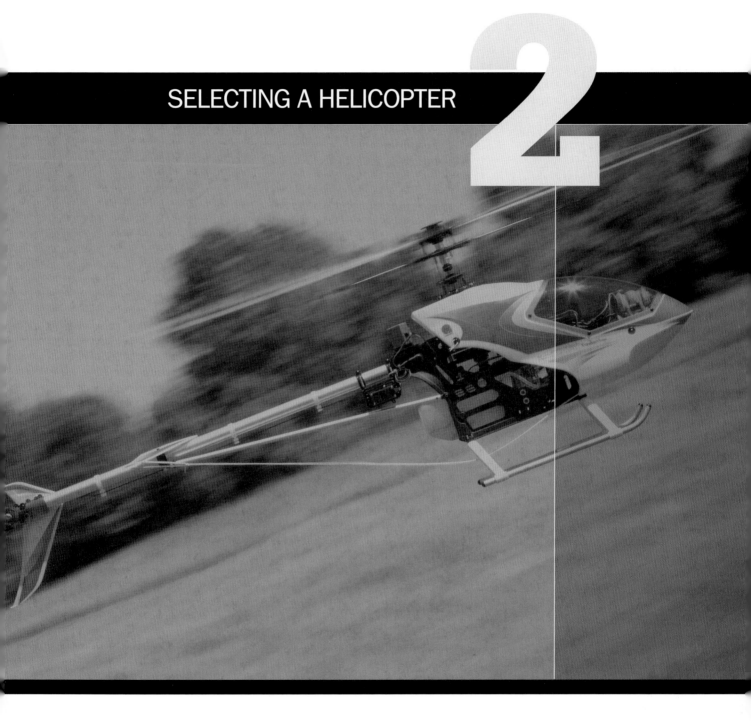

Selecting a Helicopter

Now that you've decided to buy a helicopter, you must decide exactly which one is best for you. When you look through the model magazines, you'll see a lot of choices, but each heli has advantages and disadvantages. The ads can be confusing if they use terminology that only an experienced helicopter pilot would know. So let's get familiar with some of the terms you'll come across, and then I'll discuss a few of the basic options that are available (and their limitations), so you can make the best choice.

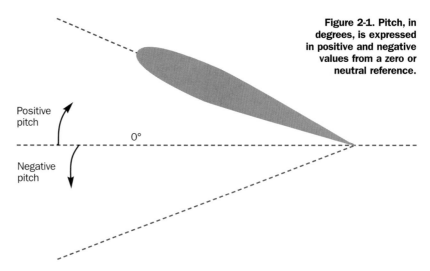

Figure 2-1. Pitch, in degrees, is expressed in positive and negative values from a zero or neutral reference.

Positive pitch

Negative pitch

0°

FIXED PITCH VS. COLLECTIVE PITCH

You'll hear "fixed pitch" and "collective pitch," and in any discussion of either, it's assumed you understand what "pitch" is. Refer to Figure 2-1; it shows the main rotor blade from the blade tip.

The angle the blade makes with a horizontal line is referred to as its pitch. This pitch angle can be:
• Negative: the leading edge of the blade is lower than the trailing edge, or
• Positive: the leading edge is higher than the trailing edge.

Pitch is measured in degrees, and the number of degrees of pitch is assumed to be positive unless it's preceded by a minus sign, e.g., -2 degrees.

If we locked this rotor blade at one specific angle, we would say it has "fixed pitch." If the rotor blade is able to move through a range of pitch angles, it has collective pitch—the ability to change its pitch angle. And, as you may already know, some helicopter designs are fixed pitch and others are collective pitch. Let's take a closer look at the advantages and disadvantages of both types.

FIXED PITCH

The main advantage of a fixed-pitch helicopter is that the rotor head is very simple. This means that the kit is less expensive to produce, the head is easier to build and repair, and repair parts will be fewer and less expensive if you need them. But what of the disadvantages?

The big disadvantage of a fixed-pitch system is the helicopter's lack of vertical control. Lift is generated by the rotor blades, and if the pitch angle is fixed, the only other way to alter lift is by varying the speed at which the blades turn (rotor rpm). And if we had a good way to adjust and maintain rotor speed,

fixed pitch might not be so bad. Unfortunately, the only way to adjust rotor speed is by increasing or decreasing engine speed, and this cannot be controlled to the degree we need.

For example, while trying to hover a fixed-pitch helicopter, you are always trying to find the correct power setting to produce the needed hover rpm. But, in reality, you either have too much power, and the helicopter climbs, or not enough power, and the helicopter descends. You therefore have to concentrate on adjusting the throttle while still paying attention to the other controls.

I'm sure many fliers have learned to hover on fixed pitch helicopters, and my comments are not meant to imply it can't be done but only that it's harder than it needs to be. Let's look at an easier system—collective pitch.

COLLECTIVE PITCH

As I mentioned, collective pitch allows you to control the pitch of the blades throughout a flight. For example, imagine another helicopter in a hover, but this one has collective pitch. To climb or descend, the engine speed and, therefore, the rotor speed, remain constant, and only a small change in the pitch of the rotor blades is required. By having the pitch, or collective, directly connected to the throttle stick, it takes only a small movement to make an almost instantaneous and minute change in the blades' pitch to climb or descend. This gives a much finer and more immediate control of the helicopter, and there's virtually no time lag between your input and the helicopter's reaction. This is just one example of the advantages of collective pitch, and although there are several more, I think you can see the immediate benefits of this type of control.

CYCLIC OR CYCLIC PITCH

The helicopter purist doesn't talk of helicopter controls as if they're airplane controls, i.e., aileron, elevator, etc., but will refer to the controls as right or left cyclic, fore and aft cyclic, etc. This is because a helicopter doesn't have an aileron or an elevator. It receives its directional control through the changing of the pitch of each blade as they complete one revolution. A good definition of cyclic

The electric-powered EF Helicopters Shogun 2 uses a fully aerobatic rotor head and can do 3D aerobatics. It can fly indoors and out.

pitch control is: "The control that changes the pitch of each individual rotor blade during a cycle of revolution to control the tilt of the rotor disc, and therefore, the direction and velocity of horizontal flight." Notice in Figure 2-2 how each rotor blade changes its pitch as it goes through one revolution. For a more detailed explanation of the changes in forces during this revolution, refer to the section on "Gyroscopic precession" in Chapter 12.

AUTOROTATION

A helicopter with autorotation capability can be controlled and brought to a safe landing even when its engine has stopped. This

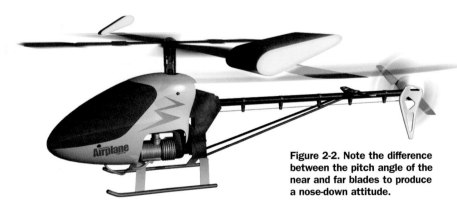

Figure 2-2. Note the difference between the pitch angle of the near and far blades to produce a nose-down attitude.

is commonly referred to as a "deadstick" landing because the engine is dead. To understand autorotation, first imagine that the helicopter does not have an autorotation capability and its engine quits during flight. Because the engine is connected to the main gear (which, in turn, is connected to both the main and tail rotors), when the engine stops, so does the entire rotor system. And obviously, once the rotor stops, the helicopter will fall out of control.

On the other hand, a helicopter with autorotation has a one-way clutch, or bearing, that allows the main rotor blades to continue to turn freely, even if the engine stops. This means that although the engine has stopped, the main rotor blades will continue to turn and thereby provide control for a landing. This is certainly a worthwhile feature, and practicing autorotation landings with the engine at idle is both a very challenging one and one that might save the helicopter.

HELICOPTER SIZE

Helicopter "size" usually refers to the size of the engine rather than to its actual physical size. The three most common sizes are the 30, 50 and 90 helicopters, so let's look at each.

.30 SIZE

Although referred to as a .30-size helicopter, almost everyone uses a .32 to .37 engine for better performance. The engine size, with a decimal in front, refers to the cubic inches of displacement. Therefore, a 30-size engine has a displacement of 0.30 cubic inch.

.50 SIZE

This is an intermediate size (between the 30- and 90-size helicopters), and many fliers use up to a 70-size engine for extreme 3D performance.

.90 SIZE

Although larger helicopters are available, this is the largest helicopter used by most fliers.

ADVANTAGES

.30

Lowest initial cost. Because .30-size helis are smaller, they are less expensive to produce.

Lowest fuel costs. Just like car engines, smaller model engines offer better fuel economy. For example, a 30-size engine requires a 6-ounce fuel tank, while a 90 will need 16 ounces. Over time, the difference in fuel cost will be substantial.

Lowest repair costs. This is actually tied to the first point—low initial cost. Because the parts are smaller and lighter, they usually cost slightly less than those of a larger helicopter.

.50

Moderate cost. As you might expect, because .50-size helis are slightly larger than .30-size birds, their prices are slightly higher, but they're still less expensive than larger helicopters.

Moderate fuel costs. Over the life of these helicopters, fuel costs will be substantially lower than those of larger helicopters, but they'll use almost twice as much fuel as smaller size copters.

Repair costs. As you would expect, repair parts cost more than the .30-size parts but less than the 90 size.

Quality. Many .50-size helicopters approach the quality of the larger machines. They can be every bit as durable and aerobatic as the larger ones.

Excess power. A 50-size engine (or larger) will provide sufficient excess power for increased climbing and overall flying performance.

.90

As the largest helicopters, these are the easiest to see when they're airborne. This is very important because if you can't see your heli, you can't control it. But no matter which size of helicopter I fly, I always prefer bright colors to stay oriented with it when it's in flight. Orientation with an airplane is generally pretty easy because of its large wing, but all we have are the fuselage area and rotor disc.

Stability. Because of their large size, .90-size helis are least affected by wind gusts.

Performance. A high-performance 90-size engine will provide maximum excess power that can be used to climb, maneuver, etc.

DISADVANTAGES

Less stable. A smaller helicopter is more susceptible to wind gusts than a larger, heavier one. If you fly in an area with light winds, this may not be an important factor, but if it's windy—more than 10 or 15mph—the smaller helicopter will be tossed about.

Less visible. A smaller helicopter is more difficult to see while it's flying. This isn't much of a problem while hovering, but once in forward flight, it cannot be flown very far away. A bright canopy and tail fin, along with a distinct rotor disc, will help.

Less performance. This size of helicopter has the least excess available power, and a helicopter performs on power.

When compared with the larger helicopters, the disadvantages of helicopters of this size are the same as those listed for the 30-size machines, although the use of a larger engine will eliminate the lack of power.

Highest initial cost. Not only are the parts larger, but designs and parts of higher quality are also required to withstand the higher loads imposed by the increased weight and power.

Fuel costs. As mentioned earlier, a 90-size engine requires a 16-ounce fuel tank, and its fuel consumption will be noticeably greater than even that of the 50-size engines.

Spare parts are more costly for the reasons already stated.

Figure 2-4. The Hirobo XRB Sky Robo Lama is fixed pitch and designed as a trainer. This electric heli can fly indoors and outside in calm weather.

Figure 2-7. The Miniature Aircraft Ion-X is a 50-size electric helicopter that's capable of every 3D maneuver.

Below: Figure 2-5. Modern helicopters such as the Raptor 50 are made almost entirely of lightweight composite material.

Figure 2-6. The Venture 50's basic framework is extremely robust.

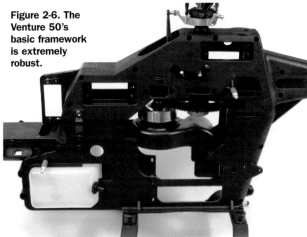

Above: Figure 2-8. A typical pod-and-boom helicopter. Note the color of the special helicopter fuel. Exhaust smoke indicates a slightly rich carburetor setting for good lubrication and engine cooling.

POD & BOOM VS. SCALE

A typical pod-and-boom helicopter is shown in Figure 2-8. The nose, which houses the radio gear, is called the pod, and an aluminum boom exits to the rear to hold the tail rotor in place. A scale helicopter is shown in Figure 2-9; it's designed to look like a full-size helicopter with a complete fuselage.

I certainly don't know the exact figures, but I imagine that about 99 percent of all the model helicopters sold are of the pod-and-boom type. They cost less than scale helicopters and are easier to assemble and repair. But pod-and-boom helicopters do have a distinct disadvantage compared with scale helicopters: they are much harder to see in flight, and that is why I recommended a bright, colorful paint scheme if possible.

When we think of flying a heli-

copter, most of us don't think of the pod-and-boom type. Instead, we see ourselves flying a scale Bell 222 with operating retracts, rotating beacons, a full scale interior, working doors and windows and (naturally) a full-scale paint job. That certainly is a commendable goal, but a project of this size should be put aside until you're a proficient flier. When you are ready for scale helicopters, they do offer very distinct advantages.

Figure 2-9. Apart from the green tape that holds the canopy on, this Bell 222 model could pass for the real thing. Note that it even has retractable landing gear. The absence of exhaust smoke indicates electric power.

Because they have large fuselages, they're easier to see and stay oriented with in flight; and those with an aerodynamic shape fly more smoothly than the pod-and-boom helicopters.

So my recommendation, at least while you're learning to fly, is to stay with a pod-and-boom helicopter until you feel very confident of your flying abilities.

CYCLIC COLLECTIVE-PITCH MIXING—CCPM

Most helicopters use one servo to control the aileron function, another for the elevator and a third for the collective pitch, and each servo acts independently of the others. An electronic CCPM (cyclic collective pitch mixing) helicopter, however, uses a combination of all three servos for aileron, elevator and collective pitch. Although there are several ways to mechanically obtain this mixing, the most common is for each servo to have one control input to the swashplate, 120 degrees from each other. Therefore, to increase the collective pitch, all three servos must move in unison to raise the swashplate an equal amount. In a similar manner, all three servos must move independently and in vary-

ing amounts to tilt the swashplate for the desired directional control. The electronic mixing required for these servo commands is generated in the transmitter, so if you are interested in a helicopter with this type of swashplate control, make sure that your radio will support CCPM mixing.

ELECTRIC HELICOPTERS

When you select a helicopter, another choice is the type of power you'll use to turn the rotor blades. As discussed, most helicopters use a model-airplane-type engine, but a growing number of electric-powered helicopters are also available. Recent advances in electric motor design, batteries, microelectronics and helicopter design and manufacturing techniques have led to the production of electric-powered helicopters with flight durations and performance we would not have thought possible a few years ago. And, since they don't need fuel or starting equipment to start an engine, electric helicopters are very quiet to operate and don't produce exhaust residue.

Size. Because electric helicopters are available in a wide variety of sizes, they are classified by the

Figure 2-10. The coning angle of the main rotor acts much like dihedral in a fixed-wing aircraft; it provides additional inherent stability in a hover.

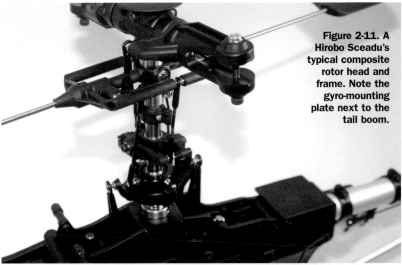

Figure 2-11. A Hirobo Sceadu's typical composite rotor head and frame. Note the gyro-mounting plate next to the tail boom.

Figure 2-12. The Freya 90 is designed for maximum performance. Plenty of room up front for battery and receiver, all push-pull controls, large visible gas tank and rear-mounted tail-rotor servo directly connected to the tail rotor. It uses a Muscle Pipe for power and an Airtronics Stylus for control.

length of their rotor blades. Mini helicopters have rotor blades in the 200 to 250mm range, while larger helicopters are compared with their gas-powered counterparts, i.e., a 50-size helicopter would have rotor blades of 550 to 600mm, while a 90 size would have rotor blades of 700mm plus.

Some smaller electric helicopters such as the Heli-Max RotoFly and E-flite Blade are completely ready-to-fly out of the box. With completely installed radio equipment, motor, mechanics, etc., they require only that their included batteries be charged for a couple of hours, and then they

are ready to fly.

And because of their small size, mini helicopters are suitable for flying indoors in a gymnasium or large garage, and outdoors in very light breezes. The larger electric helicopters are fully capable of the most extreme 3D flight and can actually exceed the flight performance of their gas-powered counterparts for 5 minutes or so.

Motors. High-performance electric motors can turn in excess of 40,000rpm, and, for short periods, can produce more power than a 90-size gas engine. It's therefore essential that the motor be cor-

rectly matched to the helicopter's flight performance and have the correct gear ratio, enough battery power and sufficient cooling during flight. Many manufacturers and hobby shops suggest a combination of helicopter, motor, gear ratio, batteries and speed control to match your flight requirements.

Speed control. A speed control is a small, electronic microprocessor that's designed to transfer electric power from the battery pack to the motor; it should be matched to the motor, battery, power requirements and size of the helicopter. Speed controls are improving rapidly, so check your local hobby shop for the latest features. As a minimum, your controller should have these safety features:

A safe-start unit will not send power to the motor until the speed control sees the receiver signal indicating that the throttle is at idle. Without this feature, the motor could immediately go to full throttle when power is applied. Not to be confused with the safe start, some speed controls have a soft-start feature that's needed when you fly fixed wings. This feature will not work on a helicopter because it's designed to accelerate the propeller slowly as power is applied.

A slow-start feature is similar to the soft start mentioned, but it's designed for helicopters. Since electric helicopters do not use a clutch system to engage the rotors, the slow start is needed on larger helicopters (550mm blades and larger) to accelerate the rotor blades slowly when power is applied.

Batteries. Several battery types are available; your choice will depend on the required level of performance, flying time and cost.

Nickel-cadmium (Ni-Cd) bat-

Figure 2-13. A colorful paint scheme makes the helicopter easier to see in flight.

teries have been used in RC equipment for many years, are relatively low in cost, can be quick-charged and provide ample power for their size and weight. Unless you want extreme aerobatic helicopter performance, Ni-Cds are a good choice for average fliers.

Nickel-metal-hydride (NiMH) batteries are slightly more expensive than Ni-Cds but offer 20 to 30 percent more capacity for a given cell size. However, owing to their high internal resistance, an additional cell may be required.

Lithium-polymer (Li-poly) and Lithium-ion (Li-ion) batteries are lighter and compared with other batteries, they produce about four times as much power for their size. Although they're expensive, they are used when maximum performance is needed.

For more information on the care and feeding of batteries, motors, speed controls, etc., I suggest that you read the appropriate volumes in the SR Batteries series on "R/C Techniques" and "E/F Techniques." Each is written in an easy-to-understand manner and contains photos and diagrams.

With such a variety of helicopters now available, you should be able to narrow your choices by evaluating the following considerations:

• Initial and operating costs. How much can you comfortably afford to spend on a helicopter and still have enough left over for the engine, radio, gyro and accessories?
• Which makes/types of helicopters are flown in your area? Ask at your hobby shop or ask other fliers for their opinions on a particular helicopter.
• Which spare parts does your hobby shop stock? No matter how many precautions you take, there will always be times when

Figure 2-14. A composite rotor head and main frames combine lightness and strength to improve flight performance.

you'll need spare parts, and it's nice to have them readily available rather than having to order them and wait several days for delivery.
• Is it better to buy a smaller, less expensive helicopter now and upgrade to a better one later? I recommend that you buy the best equipment you can comfortably afford for increased quality, performance, durability and your overall happiness while flying it.

SHOULD YOU BUY A NEW OR A USED HELICOPTER?

One drawback of a new helicopter is that most come in kit form, and you have to assemble hundreds of parts. I don't mean to imply that building a helicopter kit is difficult, because it really isn't (as we'll see later), but it does take a certain time and effort to do it right. A used helicopter is already assembled, and before buying it, you can always ask to see it fly and inspect it for damage. A helicopter in good condition without crash damage can be a good investment, since very few parts wear out with time and use.

A typical question from a prospective buyer is whether the helicopter has ever crashed. I think this is a carryover from buying used cars or model airplanes, but it really shouldn't have much bearing on a model helicopter. Even if it has crashed, its owner should have replaced the broken parts, and then it's virtually new again. But if you aren't familiar with the helicopter, ask someone who knows helicopters to inspect it for you, and then ask to see it fly. Many times, owners want to sell so they can buy a newer or better machine, and their helis may offer an excellent value to get you into this wonderful hobby.

Selecting a Radio

Now that you have an idea of the type of helicopter you'd like, the next major decision is to choose a radio-control system. If you've been looking through model magazines, you've noticed that the ads for helicopter radios are almost as confusing as those for helicopters. Let's look at some of the available options so you'll be familiar with the terms and the functions.

Those who fly RC airplanes most frequently ask whether they can use their airplane radios for their first helicopters to save money while they decide whether they really like helicopters. The answer depends on your choice of helicopter and whether you want to give up some of the extra control a helicopter radio offers.

Airplane radios are most suited to fixed-pitch helicopters because the throttle is used to change rotor rpm and, therefore, lift. If this type of radio is used in a collective-pitch helicopter, a Y-connector must be used on the receiver's throttle function to operate both the throttle servo and the collective-pitch servo. As you will see later in this chapter, this arrangement would cause you to lose a few nice-to-have features both for the engine and for the collective pitch. Although helicopter flight in this manner is possible, I recommend that you make your learning as easy as you can.

Before we get into specific helicopter radio functions, let's look at the basic differences among the

Figure 3-1. Computer radios with large display screens make setup and adjustments easy (left: JR XP9303; right: Hitec Optic 6).

radios you see advertised, whether for airplanes or for helicopters.

FM, PPM, PCM

FM—frequency modulation—produces a signal that's free of distortion (such as in your FM car radio), and the same benefit is present in RC radios. FM's capability to screen out unwanted distortion (glitches) makes this type of radio very desirable for helicopter operations.

PPM—pulse proportional mode—is similar to FM but includes an initial timing pulse. The transmitter sends this initial timing pulse to tell the receiver it's about to send further information, and then it sends additional control information in the form of a series of pulses. Each pulse corresponds to a specific channel of control, so a 6-channel radio will

have six additional pulses. The receiver then uses these pulses to control the position of each servo. This process is then repeated many times a second and is referred to as the "pulse rate." The higher the pulse rate, the more closely the servos will respond to control-stick movements. If you intend to be a serious competition flier, pulse rate could be an important consideration when you choose a radio. For the rest of us, in normal everyday helicopter flying, we couldn't tell the difference in performance from having a faster pulse rate.

PCM—pulse-code modulation—is very similar to PPM, but the initial timing pulse is now a "secretly coded pulse." The receiver will respond only to signals from the transmitter with the properly coded timing pulse and will reject signals from other sources. Currently, this is the best form of radio control, but it doesn't solve all of our problems. One characteristic of any radio-control system is that only one transmitter can operate at a time on a specific frequency. If someone else turns on a transmitter on the same frequency, the receiver would not know which signal to respond to, and whether FM, PPM, or PCM, the helicopter would eventually crash. The term for this is "being shot down." But the advantage of PCM radios is that they can fly through momentary interference (glitches) without any apparent ill effect on the helicopter because the receiver will not respond to the unrecognized signal. PCM radios usually have two options to handle interference: a hold function or a fail-safe function, and I will discuss both later. Also, if you do buy a PCM radio, make sure that the transmitter is capable of

switching from PCM to PPM for added versatility.

SELECTING A CHANNEL

We have to be careful with the word "channel." One definition would be "a specified frequency band for the transmission and reception of signals." This is much the same as when you tune your car radio to a specific station, but your car radio only receives incoming signals. With our radios, the transmitter sends control information to the receiver in the helicopter on a specific frequency (channel). This frequency is controlled by a crystal in both the transmitter and receiver, and they must be identical for the receiver to operate properly.

However, the word "channel" can also refer to the number of control functions a radio has. As an example, a 2-channel radio controls two functions—say, aileron and rudder. A 6-channel radio controls six functions, for

example, aileron, elevator, throttle, rudder, collective pitch and gyro sensitivity. Entry-level helicopter radios are available with 5 and 6 channels; more advanced radios have 10 or more channels. Although helicopters don't require more than 5 or 6 channels, radios with a greater number of channels also have better servos, more features, etc.

Before you buy a radio on a specific channel (frequency), check the following:
• The radio frequency procedures at your local flying field. Some of the smaller clubs assign each member a specific channel to guard against anyone's being shot down.
• Ask the local club members or the staff at the hobby shop whether there are problems locally with specific frequencies.

SYNTHESIZED RADIOS

A synthesized radio can transmit on any channel the pilot selects. If only the transmitter is synthe-

Figure 3-2. The Spektrum DX6 transmits on two, 2.4GHz channels to the micro, dual, 6-channel receiver mounted just above the rear landing strut. The transmitter first scans for two open channels and then transmits to the receiver, which locks on to the specific transmitter code, making the system virtually immune to interference.

Figure 3-3. Micro-receivers are well-suited to small electric helicopters as well as larger ones that have more channels. They're ideal for more sophisticated aircraft.

Figure 3-4. Servos come in a variety of sizes and specifications to suit any need.

latest RC technology, and as I write this, it is available only on the Horizon Hobby Spektrum DX6 park flyer radio. Transmitting on the 2.4GHz band, it uses the new DSSM (Digital Spread Spectrum Modulation) that allows it to simultaneously transmit and receive on two independent frequencies, so it's impervious to interference.

When the transmitter is turned on, it scans to the 2.4GHz band for two open channels and then transmits on both at the same time. The receiver is actually two micro-receivers in one; each receives one of the transmitted signals. This process takes about 5 seconds. And since the pilot has no idea which frequencies his radio is transmitting on, there's no need for frequency control at the flying field. Just turn on the radio, wait for it to find two open frequencies, and go fly.

This radio is currently limited to park flyers—small electric airplanes and helicopters with limited range. Continued improvements in this new technology should, however, make it available for use in all forms of RC in the near future.

SERVOS

Every radio manufacturer offers a wide variety of servos, and we can choose the best servo for our particular models. Although there are hundreds of available servos, they generally fall into one of three categories: standard, coreless, or digital.

Standard servo (or "sport servo"): this is a very good general-purpose servo, using a cored motor with an analog amplifier. Its main drawback is that the output shaft (the shaft that exits the top of the servo, to which the servo wheel, or arm, is attached) rotates either in a bushing or in the servo case, and this causes wear and sloppiness in con-

sized, the receiver crystal must then be changed to match the transmitter frequency. Some receivers, however, are also synthesized, making the channel-selection process much easier and faster. This is obviously a very nice feature to have if you fly at a crowded field, or if you want to fly at other fields for a contest or a fun-fly.

MODE 1 VS. MODE 2

Most helicopter pilots in the U.S. fly with control of the throttle/collective pitch and tail rotor on the left stick, leaving the aileron and elevator functions to

the right stick. This is a Mode 2 transmitter. A Mode 1 transmitter has the aileron and throttle/collective pitch on the right stick and the elevator and tail rotor on the left stick. This prevents the aileron and elevator from interfering with each other. But Mode 2 fliers like the right stick to represent the stick in a real helicopter. Either configuration works; your choice depends on your preference. Before deciding, visit your local hobby shop or talk to other helicopter pilots to see what they use.

SPREAD SPECTRUM

Spread-spectrum technology is the

trol. Therefore, this type of servo should be used only on throttle.

Most manufacturers offer upgrades to their standard servos in the form of ball-bearing versions. It's the same servo, but it now incorporates a ball-bearing-supported output shaft that provides smooth operation and extended servo life. All helicopter control functions should use ball-bearing servos.

Coreless servos are the same as standard servos except for their motors. Advantages of a coreless motor include its ability to start, stop and accelerate quicker with better torque and resolution than a cored motor.

Digital servos use a digital servo amplifier (versus the analog amplifier already mentioned), and as premium servos, they generally have a coreless motor and a ball-bearing-supported output shaft. The advantage of this type of servo is that the digital amplifier tells the motor what to do at a rate of about 300 times a second (compared with the analog amplifier's about 30 times per second). This increased processing power improves servo resolution (more accurate positioning of the arm or wheel), gives a faster control response and results in constant torque throughout the servo-travel range and increased holding power. Some digital servos are also programmable: they allow adjustments to the centering, endpoints, speed, direction of rotation and other parameters. Servo programming can be an important feature for contest fliers and the servo-matching requirements of CCPM helicopters.

The downside to the digital servo is its high power consumption. This disadvantage can, however, be minimized by using a larger battery and a battery moni-

tor and by recharging the receiver batteries prior to each flight.

Servos are also advertised as being high-torque, high-speed, ultra-precision, etc. Although these are certainly higher-quality servos, much of their increased performance isn't required when you're learning to hover and fly basic circuits. If you choose a 50-size or larger helicopter or require increased servo performance, it would be best (and less expensive) to buy these servos as part of an initial radio package. See your local hobby shop or ask other helicopter fliers for their recommendations on specific servos for your particular use and brand of radio.

A FIFTH SERVO

Most helicopter radios come with four servos, but most helicopters require five servos for proper operation. The helicopter has all the basic flight controls of an RC airplane, plus collective pitch, which is where the fifth servo is used. If your radio has four servos, buy a fifth, but it doesn't have to be a premium servo. I use this less expensive servo on the throttle where high speed and precision are not required.

THE AIRBORNE BATTERY

Rechargeable Ni-Cd batteries with a suitable charger are supplied as standard equipment with most radios. The charger is plugged into an electrical outlet and then attached to the transmitter and receiver battery packs to charge both overnight. But because the airborne battery must power the five servos usually used in a helicopter—plus the receiver and a gyro (see Chapter 5)—you'll need a large-capacity airborne battery. The abbreviation "mAh" stands for milliamp-hour, and it represents how much power the

battery is capable of providing. A 1000mAh battery has 1 amp of power, and because of the high current demands of the servos, it's the minimum I recommend for use in all except the smallest helicopters. When you use digital servos or fly 3D maneuvers, you'll need an even larger battery.

The standard Ni-Cd battery has 4 cells producing 4.8 volts, but it's also possible to use a 5-cell pack producing 6 volts. A 5-cell pack will increase servo speed and power, overcome the voltage drop of long wire lengths or poor connections and provide redundancy. If you use a 4-cell pack and 1 cell fails, you crash. With a 5-cell pack, if 1 cell fails, you simply revert to the standard 4-cell pack because Ni-Cds generally fail in a closed condition, which means that they drop out of the circuit but continue to pass the current.

Although a 5-cell pack sounds like the answer to many potential problems, it also has its disadvantages:
• You may not have the correct charger or cycler designed for use with 5 cells.
• Many believe that they can increase their flying time by using a 5-cell pack. They are mistaken. A 5-cell pack does have a greater capacity, but those faster, stronger servos draw more current and quickly deplete the battery. Therefore, as a rule, plan to have about 20 percent less useful capacity from a 5-cell pack than a 4-cell pack—just to play it safe.
• Five-cell packs are larger and heavier than 4-cell packs.
• Check your radio manufacturer's instructions or see your local dealer to make sure that your radio will operate properly on 5 cells.

Unless you need the additional servo power and speed for a large helicopter or 3D flying, I recommend that you use a standard

4-cell pack for now. And if you have any questions about your radio or helicopter battery requirements, it's better to ask questions now, rather than after a mishap.

SWITCH LAYOUT

Helicopter radios have a lot of switches and knobs, but you don't have to use them all on every flight. Nevertheless, the switch layout should be readily accessible while you're flying, so if you can, hold the transmitter and operate the switches before you buy.

HELICOPTER FUNCTIONS

Just as automobile manufacturers offer different accessories for their cars, so do RC radio manufacturers. The functions I describe aren't available on every radio, but knowing what's available will allow you to compare radios for both price and features.

All radios have certain features in common—control sticks, battery meters, charging jacks, etc.—and these functions aren't covered here but are discussed later in the book when we look at setting up a helicopter and starting to hover.

TAIL-ROTOR COMPENSATION

This feature automatically adjusts the tail rotor when the throttle/collective is increased or reduced to keep the nose pointing in the same direction. Notice the torque setup in Figure 3-5. With a clockwise-rotating main rotor blade, the torque produced by the power train and rotor blades causes the helicopter to react in the opposite direction. Remember that law of physics? For every action there is an equal and opposite reaction. Well, that applies here, and the opposite reaction to the main rotor blades will cause the helicopter nose to swing to the left. So, to keep the nose steady in a hover, engineers

Figure 3-5. Tail-rotor thrust to counter induced torque.

Blade rotation

Induced torque

invented an anti-torque device that is commonly called a tail rotor. And the function of the tail rotor is to prevent the nose from swinging to the left and to enable the pilot to move the nose right or left.

Let's imagine that the helicop-

ter is in a steady hover, and power and collective are added to make it climb. This increases the torque of the blades to the right and thereby causes the nose to react by swinging more to the left. But the tail-rotor compensation feature knows that you have added

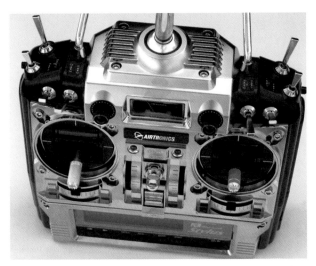

Figure 3-6. The better helicopter radios have several switches for individual functions that can be programmed to suit your needs.

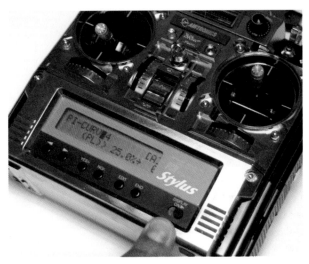

Figure 3-7. The Stylus has a display switch to allow it to be adjusted without transmitting. Note that the signal-strength meter on top of the transmitter is at zero. This is very handy for fine-tuning helicopter performance while others are flying.

power and collective and will automatically provide a little extra right rudder to keep the nose straight while the heli is climbing. In a similar manner, when descending, the torque of the main rotor blades is reduced, and this, in turn, will cause the nose to swing to the right. And again, this feature automatically reduces the tail rotor to keep the nose in a steady position.

IDLE-UP

This feature prevents the throttle from going to idle, even though the throttle stick is brought to the idle position. This is useful for aerobatics in which a low collective pitch is needed, but the engine must be kept at a high speed to maintain rotor speed. Without this idle-up feature, the engine would also be at or near idle when the throttle/collective pitch is reduced and would cause a decrease in both rotor speed and helicopter control. Most helicopter radios have more than one idle-up to allow a finer control of engine rpm over a wide range of flight parameters. I'll discuss more about this function later in the sections about landings and aerobatics.

THROTTLE HOLD

When activated, this drives the throttle to a predetermined setting (usually idle) regardless of throttle-stick position. This feature is needed to practice autorotations, and it's usual to have the throttle set to a reliable idle to simulate an engine-out condition. The collective is then controlled normally, but the engine won't respond. Again, I'll talk more about this later, when I discuss autorotations.

PITCH CURVES

This feature allows you to adjust the collective pitch relative to

control-stick input. All helicopter radios have several pitch curves that are very useful for matching the engine's power with the blades' collective pitch so that the engine isn't overloaded, while a different set of pitch curves can be used for autorotations, aerobatics, etc. For example, when using idle-up or throttle hold, each can have separate collective-pitch adjustments to optimize flight performance. As your flying skills improve, you'll be glad to have multiple pitch curves available.

DUAL RATE

This feature allows you to reduce servo throw with the flip of a

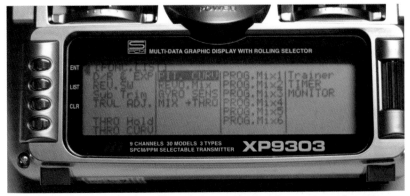

Figure 3-8. The long list of adjustable helicopter functions is easy to read on this large display. The thumb wheel on the right is used to move through the menu quickly and easily.

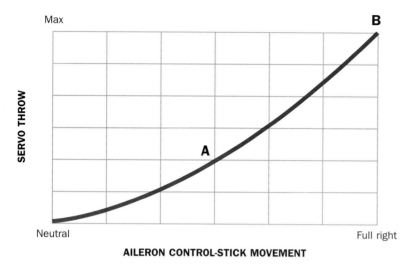

Max

B

SERVO THROW

A

Neutral

Full right

AILERON CONTROL-STICK MOVEMENT

Figure 3-9. Exponential

switch. Helicopter radios usually have dual-rate switches for aileron, elevator and tail rotor. Reduced servo throw is useful while hovering and in forward flight to avoid over-controlling, but with a flip of a switch, the dual rates are turned off, thus allowing full servo throw for aerobatics, etc.

EXPONENTIAL

This term describes how much the servo travels with respect to the amount of stick movement (see Figure 3-9). Notice that the horizontal axis depicts the amount of stick movement from neutral, while the vertical axis depicts the amount of servo travel. Starting from neutral, let's say that the stick is moved slowly to the right. A little stick movement will produce only a little servo movement, but the more we move the stick to the right, the more servo movement we get. This gives a "soft" neutral for smoother control and still allows full servo throw when the stick is moved to its extreme position. The degree of softness, or slope of the curve, can be adjusted around neutral to give you the feel you want. This feature provides soft-

ness of control around neutral for hovering and full servo travel for aerobatics—without ever moving a switch.

CCPM

As discussed in the previous chapter, this stands for cyclic collective-pitch mixing. Most helicopters use separate servos for the independent movement of the aileron, elevator and collective-pitch functions. However, with

Figure 3-10. The servo-travel endpoint is adjustable within the range indicated.

CCPM, the same three servos are each connected to a separate point on the swashplate, and their movements are mixed electronically to produce the same control results as the three independent servos. The helicopter must be specifically designed to use this type of control system, and it has the advantage of direct control between the servos and the swashplate. It therefore reduces the number of control linkages and parts count; consequently, weight is reduced. The big disadvantage, however, is that all the servos must be matched with regard to their throw and speed. If one servo reacts quicker than the others, an unwanted response to the helicopter will result.

SERVO ENDPOINT

This allows maximum servo travel to be adjusted, as shown in Figure 3-10. This is useful for matching the servo travel to a mechanical linkage in the helicopter and to equalize the response of the helicopter. For example, a helicopter with a clockwise-rotating main rotor blade will turn more easily to the right than to the left. It may therefore be beneficial to reduce right-aileron servo travel to match the right and left helicopter roll rates.

MULTI-MODEL CONFIGURATIONS

The transmitter can be programmed to fly airplanes, gliders, or helicopters, each with unique mixing functions to optimize your control of the model selected. This is especially useful when flying V-tail airplanes and helicopters using CCPM mixing.

MULTIPLE MODEL MEMORY

The transmitter will store all the flight parameters for several models with different names, so you can fly several helicopters or airplanes using one transmitter. Also, helicopter flight parameters can be stored in a second model-memory position, allowing experimental changes to be made at the field without upsetting the original model-memory parameters.

SWASHPLATE TYPE

This allows user selection of the many different types of swashplate control systems such as the CCPM already described. This increases the versatility of the transmitter because of advances in swashplate control design.

FLIGHT MODE, OR CONDITION

The transmitter can store flight parameters for several user-defined flight modes, or conditions. For example, you may name one flight condition "Hover" and all dual rates, expo-nential, pitch and throttle curves, etc., will be stored in that flight condition. Another flight condition, activated with the flip of a switch, could be defined for aerobatics, autorotation, etc., each with independent dual rates, pitch and throttle curves, etc. This greatly enhances helicopter performance for each phase of flight and is a very desirable feature.

GYRO GAIN

This allows either manual or automatic selection of different gyro gains using an independent switch or the activation of a flight mode. High gyro gains for yaw stability may be selected for hovering, while lower gyro gains may be used for aerobatics.

GOVERNOR PROGRAM

This is used with separate rpm governor systems; it allows independent rotor rpm settings for each flight mode described. This feature could be used to automatically provide a lower rotor speed for hovering, a moderate rotor speed for forward flight and an even higher rotor speed for aerobatics.

ELECTRONIC DIGITAL TRIMS

Trim switches allow minor aileron, elevator, rudder and throttle-servo adjustments during flight. If the helicopter rolls slightly to the right during a hover, instead of holding the aileron stick to the left, use a little left-aileron trim to correct this condition. And because the trims are electronic, trim rates are adjustable, so higher trim rates can be used when you fly a new model that may be greatly out of trim. Individual trim positions are also stored for each flight condition so that the left aileron trim needed for hovering may be removed when you switch to a different flight condition.

PROGRAMMABLE SWITCHES

This assigns any function to any switch. You program the transmitter to have a specific switch activate the dual rates, individual flight conditions, etc.

THROTTLE CUT

This engine-kill feature stops the engine with the push of a button. Used during an emergency or for that final autorotation of the flight, it drives the throttle to the fully closed position.

HOW ADVANCED A RADIO DO YOU NEED?

The preceding is not a complete list of helicopter-radio features, since each radio manufacturer chooses the features to include in its line of helicopter radios. This

Figure 3-11. The "Lock" button is used to lock the throttle in its present position; this is very handy when you carry the helicopter or adjust the radio while the engine is running. A similar button to kill the engine is on top of the transmitter.

should, however, give you an idea of some of the features available so that you can make an educated decision about the level of radio you would like to have. And as you can tell by looking at the various helicopter radio advertisements, there's a large variety in three basic price ranges. The least expensive are the entry-level radios; they offer all the basic functions you need for hovering and aerobatics, but they usually lack the features required for advanced aerobatics.

Intermediate radios offer a vast increase in performance for only a few dollars more. This usually includes multiple flight conditions, each containing multiple pitch and throttle curves, and other features that just make flying helicopters easier and more fun.

Top-of-the-line radios offer the most helicopter features for very precise flying, but they are quite expensive. Having made the investment, you'll find that such a radio will take you through all phases of flying and will add to your enjoyment for many years.

Buy a radio that you can comfortably afford and still have funds available for a good-quality helicopter and other equipment.

Look down the road. Which type of flying would you like to do? If you intend to stay with the hobby for several years and fly more advanced helicopters with improved flight performance, buy a radio that has the advanced features you will need.

If you "over-buy," the radio is the place to do it. It will have better transmitter and receiver electronics, high-performance digital servos and advanced features to make your flying more enjoyable.

SHOULD YOU BUY A NEW OR A USED RADIO?

A used radio that has been well cared for can be an excellent investment, especially if its price allows you to buy a more advanced radio. The transmitter and receiver are the heart of the radio, so inspect them closely for any signs of damage. Both transmitter and receiver batteries should be cycled to verify their performance because they would be expensive to replace. And if the batteries and overall appearance of the transmitter and receiver are good, a range check and function check should let you know whether they're working properly.

The servos provide the power to move all the helicopter controls, so they will wear out in time. Check every servo for its general appearance, and make sure that the mounting lugs are in good condition. Operate each servo over its entire throw range; check for smoothness of operation, and check that they all sound the same and move at the same rate.

If you don't feel comfortable doing these checks yourself, ask a more advanced flier or the staff at your local hobby shop for help. Or send the complete radio back to its manufacturer for a checkup.

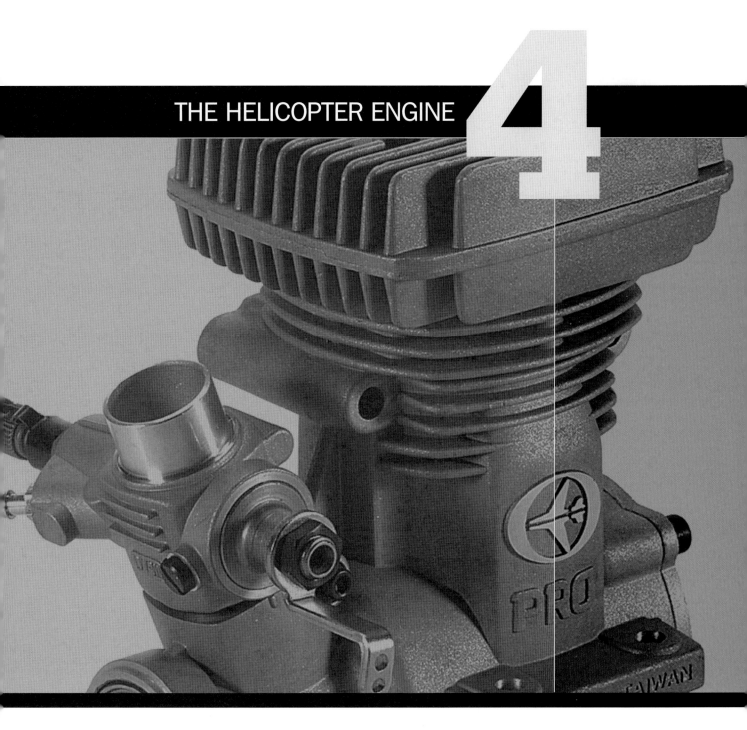

The Helicopter Engine

In Chapter 2, I discussed the three basic helicopter sizes and told you that the sizes given refer to the engine size and not to the physical size of the helicopter. And if, by now, you've decided on a helicopter size, you must now decide which engine to power it with. Choosing an engine can be confusing because not only are there different sizes and brand names, but there are also different types of carburetors, port arrangements, metals used in construction, etc. Let's look at some of your options.

Figure 4-1. The SH 37 and the Magnum 52 are typical helicopter-engine designs. They have large heat-sink heads and easy-to-adjust carburetors.

ENGINE REQUIREMENTS

One of the most basic differences between a helicopter and almost any other form of aircraft is that a helicopter relies exclusively on power for flight. An airplane may need power from an engine to climb, but once at altitude, it can be powered back and will glide on the lift produced by its wings. Although the rotor disc of a helicopter is much like the wing of an airplane in many respects, it always needs power to keep it rotating to provide this lift. This makes a helicopter completely dependent on its engine, which, therefore, must be very powerful and reliable.

This is why most fliers will ensure that they have more than adequate power for their helicopters. The other advantage of slightly over-powering your helicopter with a larger engine is that the fuel mixture can be set slightly rich. Although a rich mixture will cause a slight loss of

power, the engine will run cooler and be better lubricated, so it will last longer and be more reliable. I mention improved lubrication because the engine receives its lubrication only from the fuel, and if you run it lean to get maximum power, it could be slightly too lean, and that will cause overheating, engine damage and possibly engine failure in flight.

One of the first things you'll notice in the magazine ads is the large number of engine manufacturers producing engines for both airplanes and helicopters. Before you choose an engine, go to the local flying field and see which engines are most popular. Talk to some of the fliers, observe whether they fly airplanes or helicopters, and ask whether they'd recommend their engines for your helicopter. Buy a top-of-the-line engine if you can afford it, as this is the basic piece of equipment that keeps your helicopter away from the ground.

HEAT-SINK HEAD

Usually, a helicopter engine comes with a large heat-sink head to aid cooling because, unlike on an airplane, the engine isn't in a free airstream.

INTAKE AND EXHAUST

In Figure 4-1, you'll see front-intake engines with side exhausts. The front intake means that the carburetor is mounted on the front of the engine rather than on the backplate behind the engine. As well as having a side exhaust, some engines also come with a rear exhaust that again exits at the back of the engine. Although some helicopters may use a rear-intake/rear-exhaust engine, most are designed for the front-intake and side-exhaust engine.

CARBURETOR

Most model engines have a 2-needle carburetor. The main needle valve, as its name implies, is used to adjust how much fuel enters the engine. The idle needle valve is used to further adjust the fuel mixture when the engine is at idle. However, because helicopters spend a lot of time hovering at less than full throttle, many helicopter engines come with a carburetor that's designed specifically for midrange operation. These carburetors have a third, or midrange, needle valve. And to ensure that the carburetor always has enough fuel, some engines also have a fuel pump, or demand regulator.

As you progress towards more advanced aerobatics and 3D-type maneuvers, you may well need the advantages of these more advanced engines and carburetors, but they are not required for "normal" helicopter performance. The addition of fuel pumps, regulators, more needle valves, etc. increases the complexity of adjusting an engine and should be used only when improved flight performance is required.

ENGINE BREAK-IN

Today's engines are of such a high quality that they require very little, if any, break-in prior to use. But read the engine manufacturer's instructions carefully, and, if you can, break the engine in on your workbench with a propeller attached. If that is not possible, run several tanks of fuel through the engine in your helicopter before you require maximum power on a continuing basis. In a later chapter, I will go over how to properly set the engine mixture and throttle, but your engine instructions should be good enough for you to get it started and broken in. Again, if there are other modelers in your area, I'm sure they'll be glad to help you.

IN-FLIGHT MIXTURE ADJUSTMENT

Some engines have an optional carburetor that can adjust the fuel mixture while the helicopter is flying. These carburetors aren't very popular in the United States but are used extensively in other parts of the world. Although they are not well advertised, you should at least consider one for your helicopter.

One of the difficulties with adjusting the fuel mixture is that the engine can't be tested under load until the helicopter is taken to a hover or is flying. If the mixture is slightly off, the helicopter must be landed and the mixture readjusted. Do this at the beginning of each flying session because changes in temperature, humidity, etc., will slightly affect

Figure 4-2. The O.S. Max 50 SX-H Hyper has a unique head design with more cooling area. The carburetor includes high, low and mid-range mixture adjustments to allow extremely accurate settings.

the engine's mixture requirements. Small changes, however, can be accomplished quickly and easily with an in-flight mixture adjustment. Not all engines are available with an in-flight-adjustable carburetor, so check with your dealer before ordering.

If you intend to use in-flight mixture adjustment, you'll also need an extra servo, and I suggest one of the small, inexpensive servos because compared with the other servos, it will be used much less frequently and won't have as much of a load placed on it. To make small mixture adjustments,

your radio also needs a spare channel that's controlled by a knob or a trim lever rather than a switch.

PISTON DESIGN

The piston must create a seal with the cylinder to compress the fuel/air mixture before it will ignite. This seal is created by using a ring like that used in our car engines or by having such a tight piston-to-cylinder fit that a ring isn't needed.

THE RINGED ENGINE

As already mentioned, this engine uses a ring like the one in your car engine. This has long been the standard way of ensuring a seal between the piston and the cylinder, and it has the advantage of moderate compression that can be turned over, or started, by the average electric starter. After many hours of use, the ring may wear and need to be replaced, but with a minimum of work and expense, the engine can be brought back to an almost new condition. Because of these features, most helicopter engines are ringed.

THE ABC ENGINE

ABC stands for aluminum, brass and chrome (of which the piston and cylinder are made). When this type of engine is cold, it has a great deal of compression and requires the strongest electric starter to turn it over. But once started and brought up to operating temperature, the three metals expand at different rates to produce the correct amount of compression without the use of a ring. Because this type of engine is designed to run at peak operating temperatures, it can withstand the abuse of a lean run better than a ringed engine can.

Engine manufacturers are also experimenting with other metal combinations, but the design and general handling characteristics of these engines should be about the

Figure 4-3. Designed to maximize performance, Curtis Youngblood Muscle Pipes are available for 30-, 50- and 90-size engines. Their workmanship is outstanding.

same as already described. Again, see your local hobby dealer for his recommendation on an engine that will meet your helicopter and flying requirements.

GLOW PLUGS

A glow plug serves the same purpose as the spark plug in our cars: to supply the fire to ignite the fuel/air mixture. The glow plug, however, glows initially when connected to a 1.5V battery during engine starting, and it continues to glow (without the battery) because of the heat of combustion during engine operation.

Glow plugs are available in long and short versions, and engine manufacturers recommend specific plugs for their engines. Your local hobby shop folks will recommend one for the engine/fuel combination you use.

FUEL

Your final choice is which fuel to use with your engine/glow-plug combination. Model engine fuel is generally composed of methanol (which burns and provides the power), nitromethane (which is a power additive and also provides a more reliable idle) and castor oil or synthetic oil for lubrication. Although you don't have an option with the methanol, you can choose the type of lubrication and the percentage of nitromethane (nitro).

Your engine will provide more than sufficient power for your initial hovering, so burning a high percentage of nitro will merely increase the cost of fuel without giving any noticeable benefits. Small amounts, however, will improve idle characteristics, so I recommend something in the 5- to 15-percent-nitro range. As you progress and become used to your engine's handling, try fuels that have various percentages of nitro to match fuel costs with engine/helicopter performance.

Because we use 2-stroke engines, we must mix oil with the fuel to provide engine lubrication. Many years ago, the only lubrication was castor oil. This was excellent, especially at the higher temperatures associated with a "lean run," but it left deposits inside and outside the engine. Synthetic oils were developed that burn clean and do not leave such deposits, but they aren't as good as castor oil at higher operating temperatures.

So, now the choice: castor or synthetic or a combination of both? And how much lubricant should be in the fuel? Because your initial hovering will not require maximum engine power, it can be set slightly rich, thereby keeping the engine out of the high-temperature range. I recommend a minimum of 20-percent synthetic oil, or a mixture of castor and synthetic. Using less

than 20-percent oil will increase power and improve fuel economy, but it could well be inadequate lubrication for reliable engine operation and long engine life.

MUFFLER OR TUNED MUFFLER?

Most helicopter engines are not supplied with a muffler as standard equipment because they require different muffler systems. Engines that do come with a muffler (notably airplane engines) are generally unsuitable for helicopters because they're designed for horizontal installation in an airplane; that is, the engine crankshaft is in a horizontal position, and the muffler exhausts to the rear. In a helicopter, however, most engine installations are vertical and require the muffler to be at 90 degrees to the crankshaft.

A muffler does exactly what its name implies: it muffles engine noise. Unfortunately, it also detracts from its performance. Manufacturers have therefore combined the benefits of a tuned pipe (which increases engine performance) with a muffler to produce a tuned muffler (see Figure 4-3). They do an excellent job of improving, or at least maintaining, engine performance while muffling engine sound.

Since you will not need maximum engine performance for your initial flights, you can use a muffler or a tuned muffler, depending on your engine, fit to your helicopter, cost, etc. Your helicopter instructions may recommend a specific muffler that's designed for it, or your local hobby shop can recommend a suitable aftermarket alternative.

THE GYRO **5**

The Gyro

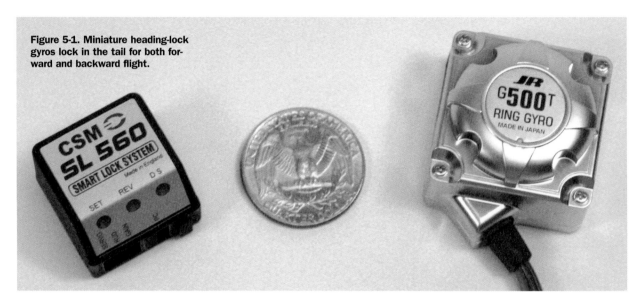

Figure 5-1. Miniature heading-lock gyros lock in the tail for both forward and backward flight.

The gyro is the last of the RC helicopter's four essential components. Connected between the receiver and the tail-rotor servo, the gyro senses any non-requested nose movement (right or left) and sends a corrective signal to the servo (without being directed by the receiver) to counter that nose movement.

The first gyros used heavy spinning wheels to produce the gyroscopic force from which the gyro gets its name. Battery power was required to keep these wheels spinning, and once spinning, they tried to maintain their positions. Any yaw motion of the helicopter about the vertical axis would be felt by the wheels and would cause them to tilt. This tilting was picked up by the gyro electronics and converted into a command to the tail-rotor servo to counter the helicopter's yaw movement.

Improvements in microelec-

tronics have given birth to the solid-state gyro: a gyro without moving parts. It's beyond my scope here to describe the electronics involved. What's important to us is that the new gyros are compact, they should last longer (because there aren't any spinning wheels), they use much less electrical power, they're much less susceptible to crash damage, and they're much more sensitive to yaw movement.

From this brief, non-technical explanation, we see that the gyro has no function unless the nose of the helicopter moves from side to side, and only then does the gyro command the tail-rotor servo to try to stop that movement. At first, novice pilots may think: "I won't let the nose swing in either direction, and I can therefore avoid buying a gyro." Although that sounds like a good solution, let's take another look at our helicopter in a hover. Small changes

in cyclic or collective pitch are constantly required to keep the helicopter in position, and with those changes comes a change in the helicopter's torque. This change in torque will cause the nose to swing right and left—sometimes rather quickly and violently, especially if the helicopter isn't trimmed properly. You can certainly control these nose movements, but it will require a great deal of attention and quick, accurate tail-rotor inputs to keep the helicopter pointing in one direction. And this is where the gyro comes in. It immediately senses yaw and makes an input to the tail-rotor servo in the opposite direction. The amount of gyro input, or sensitivity, is adjustable and will be discussed in a later chapter when I talk about the helicopter setup.

There are two basic types of gyro: the rate gyro and the heading-hold (or lock) gyro. To better understand the differences between the two, let's look at a hovering helicopter, but this time, it's in a crosswind that causes it to yaw in the direction of the oncoming wind.

The rate gyro senses the initial yaw movement into the wind and sends a signal to the tail rotor to stop the yaw. Once the yaw movement has been stopped, the gyro signal to the tail rotor is also stopped. Since the helicopter is continually exposed to the crosswind, it again starts to yaw, and again, the gyro sends a command to stop the yaw. But since the gyro does not send a command to the tail rotor until it detects a yaw movement, it's always a little late in its command, and although the gyro will stop the yaw movement, it never returns the nose to its original position. This characteristic can be reduced by increasing the gain of the gyro (so the sensitivity of the gyro is increased to more quickly detect yaw move-

ment and send a correcting command to the tail rotor), but too much gain will cause the tail to hunt or wag, so the gain adjustment has its limits. And if the crosswind continued, the helicopter's nose would eventually turn in the direction of the wind.

Gyros usually have dual rates controlled by a spare radio channel and selected by a transmitter switch that allows the pilot to select a high gyro gain and a lower gyro gain. In one switch position, the gyro will be in high gain rate to keep the nose steady while hovering; in the other switch position, the gyro will be in a lower gain rate for normal flying or aerobatics. Each gyro rate position can be adjusted to suit your particular helicopter and flight requirements.

Rate gyros should also incorporate a stick-priority feature. Manufacturers have various names for this feature, but stick priority basically tells the gyro not to interfere with the pilot's com-

mands to the tail rotor. Without this feature, the gyro would try to counter the yaw commands given by the pilot, and that would require larger tail-rotor commands both to overcome the gyro and to turn the helicopter as desired.

The heading-hold (lock) gyro operates in exactly the same way as the rate gyro, but it not only stops the helicopter's yaw movement but also returns the nose to its original position. Using the example of the helicopter hovering in a crosswind, the helicopter's nose will now remain stationary and will not turn in the direction of the wind. Also, unlike the rate gyro, once the heading-hold gyro returns the helicopter to its original position, it does not stop giving commands to the tail-rotor servo but continues the commands to keep the nose in the specified position.

More advanced heading-hold gyros also employ a "yaw rate demand" feature. This type of

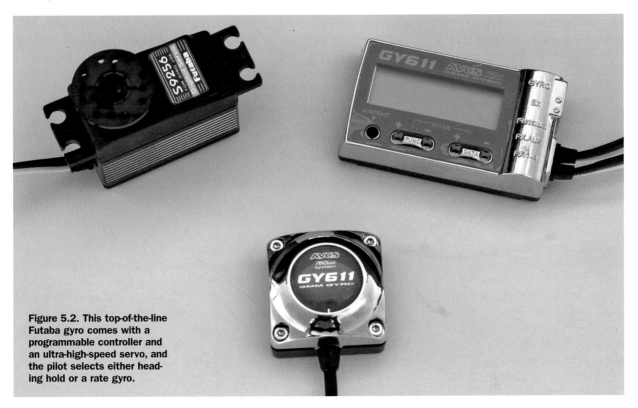

Figure 5.2. This top-of-the-line Futaba gyro comes with a programmable controller and an ultra-high-speed servo, and the pilot selects either heading hold or a rate gyro.

Figure 5-3. The CSM heading-hold gyro (left) looks almost lost next to the supplied computer cable and disc for advanced programming.

gyro interprets the pilot's tail-rotor inputs as requests for the gyro to establish a specified yaw rate. The gyro will then drive the tail-rotor servo to whichever position is needed to establish this commanded yaw rate. This means that the helicopter will turn equally well to the right and the left, even when hovering in a crosswind. This is certainly a nice feature to have in a gyro.

Although the heading-hold gyro seems to be ideal, it has higher requirements both of the battery and of the tail-rotor servo. Heading-hold gyros have very high frame rates (compared with rate gyros) for more precise control inputs to the tail-rotor servo. This will cause the tail-rotor servo to start and stop very abruptly and to make large control movements to meet the independent demands of the gyro. This servo must therefore be of the highest quality and extremely fast—able to travel 60 degrees in $\frac{1}{10}$ second or less. This extremely fast servo movement will also strain the servo motor, require a lot of bat-

tery power and produce a great deal of heat. It is therefore imperative that the servo and battery be matched to meet the gyro requirements.

In an attempt to improve gyro/servo performance, pilots have turned to battery packs with higher voltages. But this higher voltage will certainly push the servo to its design and performance limits and very possibly limit its service life. So, unless you progress to 3D-type flying or otherwise require maximum performance from your helicopter, I recommend that you stay with a standard 4-cell, 4.8V Ni-Cd battery pack. Also, if you want to change to a battery pack with a higher voltage, check the power specifications of the receiver, gyro and servo to make sure that they're designed to handle this extra voltage.

Heading-hold gyros also have many of the following features:
• Pilot selectable in-flight modes between a rate gyro and a heading-hold gyro.
• Pilot selectable in-flight dual

rates to optimize helicopter performance.
• Independent adjustable yaw-rate gain for both right and left stick deflection. This can be used to match the helicopter's right and left yaw rates.
• Adjustable control delays for starting and stopping yaw commands to prevent tail overshoot and waggles in the tail rotor.
• Changing flight modes in flight to optimize gyro performance for 3D or normal flight.
• Linkage-limit adjustment to trim the tail-rotor servo endpoints and prevent mechanical binding.
• High frame rates to optimize digital-servo performance.

No matter which type of gyro/servo combination you choose, they will require battery power to operate. Although the gyro itself uses very little power, it can send up to 3 amps to the servo for max performance maneuvering at high gain rates. Therefore, a battery with a larger capacity than is usually supplied with the radio is almost essential. Larger batteries also mean an increase in weight that hinders helicopter performance, so there are practical limits to the size of battery pack that can be used. Helicopters with rate gyros performing normal flight maneuvers should do well with a 1000mA battery pack, while heading-hold gyros and more aggressive maneuvering may well require a 2000mA (or larger) battery pack. Also, no matter which size of battery pack you use, it should be checked before flight (as described in a later chapter). Batteries are available in sizes to handle almost any requirement, so check the gyro and servo instructions or see your local dealer for the exact battery requirements.

ACCCESSORIES 6

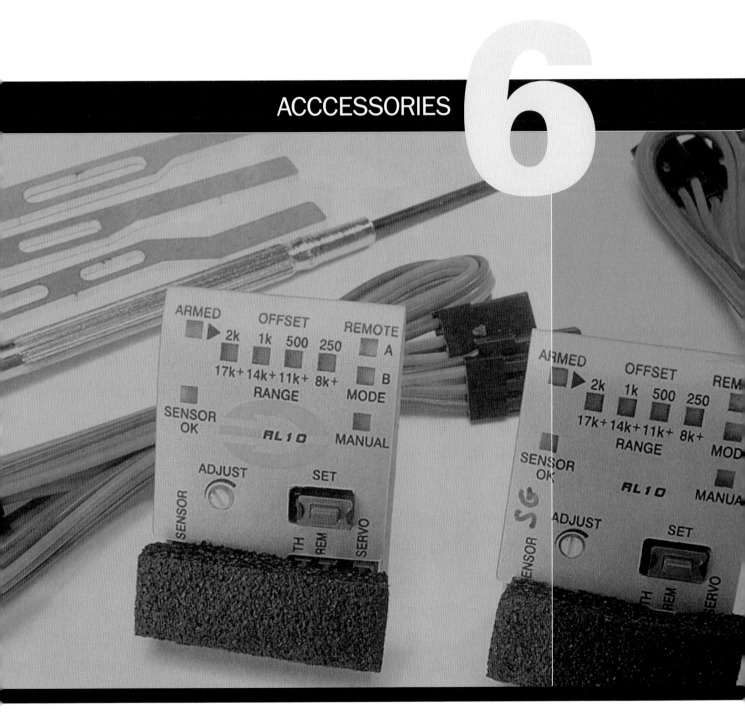

Accessories

Having discussed the essential parts of a helicopter system, it's now time to consider the support equipment, or accessories, that you'll need to operate it successfully. You don't have to buy all of these right away, but you'll need many of them as you build and practice. You can buy the accessories at your local hobby shop or through the Internet; you may even find someone who has used equipment for sale. But before you buy, be sure the part will fit your helicopter, engine, etc.

NECESSARY ACCESSORIES

A fifth servo. Collective-pitch helicopters require a fifth servo, and you'll need one as you build the helicopter. If you use a rate gyro and your servos perform sufficiently well to use on the tail rotor (as described in the previous chapter), the fifth servo can be of a lesser quality than the other servos. Use this less expensive servo on the throttle, where it will be subjected to less strain and wear.

If you intend to use a heading-hold gyro, your tail-rotor servo must be very fast, so check the gyro's instructions for their minimum servo requirements. If servo specifications aren't available, choose a digital servo that has a speed of about 0.10 second (for 60 degrees of travel) and is compatible in size and strength with your other servos. Also, make sure that the servo's connector is compatible with your receiver and gyro connections.

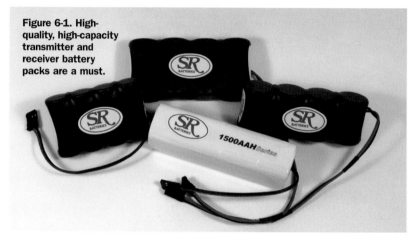

Figure 6-1. High-quality, high-capacity transmitter and receiver battery packs are a must.

A large airborne battery. If your radio and gyro are designed to be powered by one battery, you may need a battery with a larger capacity than the one supplied with your radio. This battery has to power five servos (some or all of which may be digital servos) as well as the gyro, and must also have a safety reserve. I recommend at least a 1000mAh battery, and an 1800mAh would be even better. Again, make sure that it comes with a connector that's compatible with your receiver connections.

A muffler. If you haven't bought one to fit your helicopter/engine combination, this is the time to do it. Right now, you don't need maximum power from your engine, but you will be spending a lot of time very close to the helicopter and possibly practicing in your backyard or near other people, so quietness is definitely desirable. As your flying skills improve, however, you will benefit from the extra power offered by a tuned muffler, many of which are also very quiet.

Metric or standard hex and nut drivers, depending on the type of nuts and bolts used on your heli-

Figure 6-2. Ball-link pliers make short work of disconnecting ball links.

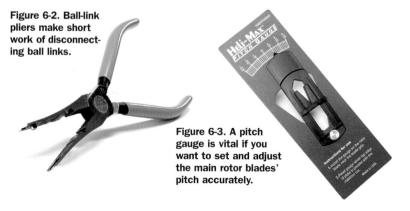

Figure 6-3. A pitch gauge is vital if you want to set and adjust the main rotor blades' pitch accurately.

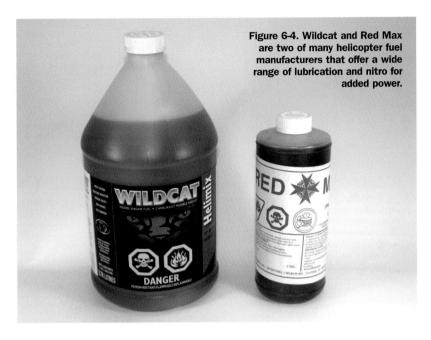

Figure 6-4. Wildcat and Red Max are two of many helicopter fuel manufacturers that offer a wide range of lubrication and nitro for added power.

Nitromethane increases your engine's power and improves its idle capability. Anywhere from 5 to 15 percent should be fine while learning to hover and fly, but 30 percent is used by many pilots who want maximum engine power. And, as you practice, try a variety of fuels to see whether your engine responds better to one than another. Some manufacturers also offer a special helicopter blend; you'll immediately notice its color. It's usually darker to make it more visible, and it's blended for a more mid-range engine operation. Manufacturers claim that its ingredients will increase power, decrease varnish buildup, decrease fuel-tank foaming and give an excellent idle and throttle response. Those I've tried give excellent results.

copter. You'll use these throughout the building process and when you go flying. You might be able use a set of hex wrenches to turn the bolts and a pair of pliers to hold the nut, but I would not recommend it. A ball hex driver is also a must if you're to adjust some hard-to-reach bolts while at the flying field. Check with your local hardware store or hobby shop for a set with large slip-free grips; they should also be long enough to get into tight places and of high quality to last many years.

Ball-link pliers. These special pliers for disconnecting the ball links aren't absolutely necessary because you could get by with a pair of needle-nose pliers. But they make disconnecting the ball links a lot easier, and you will be doing a lot of that as you build and adjust your helicopter. I recommend a high quality pair.

You'll use a pitch gauge quite often, at home and at the field, to set and adjust the pitch of the main rotor blades. I recommend one of high quality that is large and easy to read and is adjustable to suit a variety of blade sizes.

A balancer for the rotor blades, head, etc. The most accurate rotor-blade balancer is the Koll RotorPro balancer from Miniature Aircraft, and it's the only one that can balance all types of rotor blades in both chordwise and spanwise CG. When they're used with a digital gram scale (available at office supply stores), even the balance of ready-to-fly blades can be checked and adjusted for optimum smoothness and performance. You'll need an additional balancer to balance the main shaft and the rotor head.

Fuel. Your hobby shop should be able to recommend a brand that's suitable for your engine and climate. Conventional model-engine fuel contains about 70 percent methanol (methyl alcohol, which burns and gives you power), about 20 percent synthetic oil or castor oil (which doesn't burn, but lubricates and helps to cool the engine) and about 10 percent nitromethane (which aids combustion).

Most fuels contain 5 to 30 percent nitromethane, but those for use in racing engines may have as much as 65 percent.

Fuel pump and tubing. Now that you have the fuel, you need a way to get it into your fuel tank. Several types of mechanical and electrical pumps are available; you

Figure 6-5. You'll need an electric starter and a starter extension.

Figure 6-6. The Equalizer Flightdeck will take care of all your power needs at the flying field.

Figure 6-7. RotoPod training gear make a wide base that's well away from the ground to protect your helicopter while you learn to hover.

Figure 6-8. Hirobo training gear replace the stock gear on the Sceadu 30.

Figure 6-9. Modern electronics take care of our batteries.

Figure 6-10. Battery monitors take the guesswork out of batteries and are available for airborne as well as field batteries.

Figure 6-11. High capacity Li-poly batteries require special chargers.

Figure 6-12. New advances in electronics allow receiver batteries to be more precisely monitored.

may see them being used at your local flying field, and that will help you to make your decision about which to use. You'll also need several feet of fuel tubing for the tank connections to the engine, and to get the fuel from the pump to your fuel tank. Fuel tubing is available in several colors to match your helicopter, etc.

A fuel filter. To trap small dirt particles, many fliers install a fuel filter between the fuel tank and the engine. I prefer to have the filter on the fuel-can line. Extra care here might prevent small particles from clogging the carburetor.

An air filter. Because you'll spend a lot of time with the engine running close to the ground, this precaution may extend your engine's life by keeping the dirt out of it.

An electric starter will be needed to start the engine. If your helicopter is started from the top, you'll also need a starter extension to connect the starter to the start shaft on the helicopter. I don't like the "hex" starter extensions because they turn when they're being disengaged from the start shaft, and they can therefore spin into the head and surrounding links. I prefer a starter extension with a one-way bearing; this allows the starter to come to a

stop before it's disengaged from the start shaft. Also, if you've decided on a 60-size engine or larger and it's an ABC type, you'll need a very hefty starter/battery combination to turn it over.

A 12V battery and charger are required to power the starter and other electrical accessories. I recommend a large motorcycle battery or the FlightDeck by Equalizer; either will take care of all your electrical needs at the field. There's nothing worse than having to stop flying in the middle of a beautiful day because your battery went dead and you can't start the engine or quick-charge your batteries, etc.

A power panel or a 1.5V battery. To start the engine, you must provide 1.5 volts of electricity to make the glow plug "glow." When the engine is running, the heat of combustion is enough to keep the plug glowing. You can provide this power with an individual 1.5V battery or a power panel—an electrical panel used to power the glow plug, electric fuel pump, electric starter, etc. There are several types available, and new designs come on the market all the time. Some have a meter to show that the glow plug is good and can recharge a 1.5V glow-plug battery; some have a rheostat to vary the amount of current going to the plug, and others are completely automatic. This power panel and a freshly charged 12V battery will keep you fueling, starting and flying all day.

Connectors. Depending on whether you decide on a power panel or a standalone 1.5V battery, you'll need the electrical cables to connect the battery to the glow plug, to the electric fuel pump and to any other accessories. The proper connectors for the power panel are usually supplied with the unit, but you'll need connectors for the glow plug. Again, your local hobby dealer can make suggestions.

Spare glow plugs and a wrench. If you supply too much voltage to the glow plug or run your engine too lean, or if the plug just wears out, you'll have to replace it. In this case, you'll need a spare plug and a 5⁄16 socket driver to install it.

Field box. Now that you have a fairly good supply of accessories, you need something in which to transport them to the field. Special field boxes hold your power panel at a convenient angle and provide space for the fuel can, electric starter, etc. If you're a competent woodworker, you might prefer to design and build your own field box to suit your needs.

Training gear. You'll need some form of training gear to attach to your helicopter to prevent it from tipping over during your initial attempts at hovering. Several types of training gear are available commercially, and you can build your own. The best commercial version I've seen is the RotoPod (Figure 6-7). It allows the helicopter to rotate freely, and it keeps it well off the ground to prevent a "boom strike" (when the main rotor blades contact the tail boom and damage both).

You can also make your own set of training gear with 3- to 4-foot lengths of wooden dowel (sold at your local lumberyard and building-supply store). One-half inch should be enough for 30-size helicopters, and 5⁄8 inch should be fine for 60-size helicopters. Inexpensive, easy-to-attach, plastic "wiffle" balls are available at sporting-goods stores and others. Attach them to the ends of the dowels to prevent the dowels from digging into the ground. Cross two dowels in the form of an X, and attach them to your helicopter skids with rubber bands and with the crossing point under the main shaft. For a sturdier design, use four lengths of dowel and set them about a foot apart with two pointing north to south and the other two pointing east-west. It will now

resemble a tic-tac-toe design. Attach the crossing points to the front and rear of each skid with rubber bands.

Glue/filler. Something always needs to be fixed at the flying field—on your helicopter or someone else's. Instant cyanoacrylate (CA) glue with accelerator, or quick-set epoxy is nice to have on hand. I like the type that hardens in 3 minutes when exposed to sunlight.

Spare nuts, bolts, etc. The helicopter's manufacturer will supply all the nuts and bolts required for assembly, but there's always a good reason to have spares on hand. Parts might loosen, break because of fatigue, or get lost while you're disassembling the helicopter for cleaning and repair. In any case, a modest supply of the most common nuts, bolts and washers will come in handy.

A table and chair. Although they aren't really accessories, I recommend that you take a table and a chair to the flying field. You can use the table to keep the helicopter off the ground when you clean and inspect it between flights and when adjust it and make minor repairs. Putting your helicopter on a table will protect it from being stepped on and will allow others to see it properly.

Figure 6-13. Connect the CBA II to a computer, and it will provide (and save) easy-to-read graphs of your battery's discharge performance.

Figure 6-14. Carbon-fiber tail-rotor blades by V-Blades complement the other carbon-fiber parts.

Figure 6-15. High performance V-Blades and Thunder Tiger composite blades are protected in this Heli-Max case.

Figure 6-16. A frequency checker will let you know which frequencies are in use—especially helpful when you fly somewhere other than a club field.

USEFUL ACCESSORIES

An increasing number of accessories make modeling easier and more enjoyable. The following are in the "nice-to-have" category. This might be a nice wish list for holiday or birthday presents.

Battery chargers, checkers and cyclers. Batteries continue to be the weak link in our radio systems, and many manufacturers have developed products that enable us to monitor battery performance more closely and that warn us before a bad battery causes a crash. These include fast field chargers to top off batteries between flights, battery cyclers and onboard voltage and power indicators.

Rotor blades. Rotor blades come in a variety of sizes, shapes and prices. Basic wooden blades have been used for years and are still available for hovering and normal flying. Fiberglass and other composite blades offer improved

aerobatic performance, are virtually bolt-on and fly with little, if any balancing or additional work, but they cost more. A rotor-blade carrying case will also protect the blades from being damaged in storage and when being transported.

Rev limiter. This is used to regulate the maximum rpm of the engine/rotor to prevent an overspeed.

Rev lock. It's similar to the rev limiter, but now the engine is controlled to maintain a given engine speed and, therefore, rotor speed.

Lights. External running lights are powered by the airborne battery, are very bright, make the helicopter easier to see in the air and add a unique look.

Frequency checker. This will allow you to check whether someone else is transmitting on any RC airborne frequency. This is especially nice to have when you fly at an uncontrolled flying site such as a park or in your backyard where no one is monitoring the frequencies in use.

Auto-pilot/copilot. This combination fail-safe receiver and external sensors mounted on the helicopter will automatically bring the helicopter back to straight and level flight when the transmitter control sticks are released.

Whip antenna. A short, base-loaded antenna can replace the usual several feet of receiver-wire antenna.

Remote glow-plug adapter. Helicopters usually have their engines buried inside the main frame, and it's difficult, if not impossible, to get to the glow plug to start the engine. One end of this adapter

snaps onto the glow plug while the other end can be mounted on the side of the helicopter, making it easy to attach the glow plug battery for starting.

Spare parts. Although no one likes to think about crashing, it does unfortunately happen, and it's best to be prepared with a basic set of spare parts that will help you to get back into the air in a hurry. It always seems that if I crash, it happens late on a Saturday afternoon, and if I don't have the spare parts on hand, I won't be able to fly the next day. Here are a few helicopter items to keep on hand.

A set of main-rotor and tail-rotor blades; main gear; tail boom; canopy and fin set; main shaft, blade spindle

There are many other items you might want to keep in stock, but these basics will get you back into the air in a hurry.

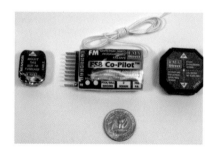

Figure 6-17. The Co-Pilot is an extremely small, light, flight-stabilization system that will return your helicopter to level flight.

Figure 6-18. A transmitter tray with a neck strap supports the weight of the transmitter and your hands, so you can make more precise control inputs.

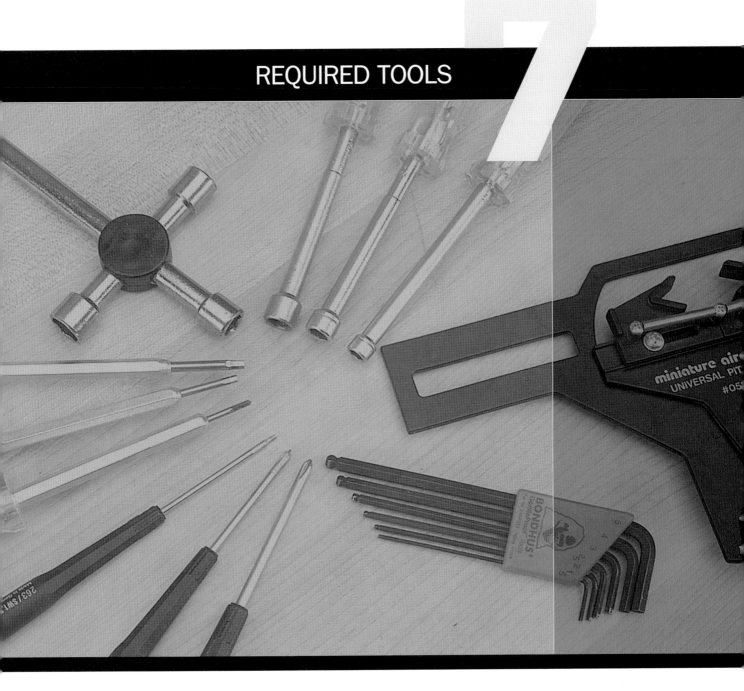

Required Tools

L ike the Erector set I had when I was a boy, most helicopters require the joining of many parts with what seem like thousands of screws, bolts, nuts and pieces of different sizes. Assembly doesn't require many sophisticated tools, and you probably already have most of them in your workshop. You should check my list to be sure you have at least the essentials; you can set them aside in a special toolbox.

BASIC TOOLS

Pliers. A pair of standard pliers and needle-nose pliers with a 90-degree bend are very helpful for reaching into tight spots.

Screwdrivers. Get a set of both standard and cross-point, or Phillips, types in medium and small. High quality and hardened tips will make these a pleasure to work with. By rubbing them with a magnet, you can magnetize them to hold small screws.

A set of hex drivers, ball hex drivers (for getting into those hard-to-reach places) and nut drivers. Your helicopter will use standard or metric parts, so check which tools you will need. And as with the screwdrivers, high quality and hardened tips are worth the money.

Hobby knife with a variety of small blades.

Metric ruler for use with helicopters that have parts in metric measurements.

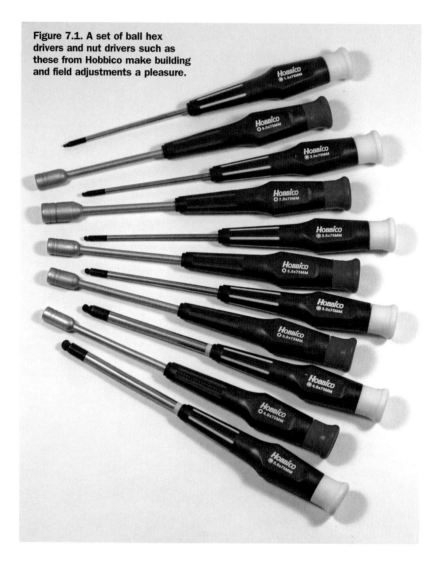

Figure 7.1. A set of ball hex drivers and nut drivers such as these from Hobbico make building and field adjustments a pleasure.

Electric drill. The cordless, variable-speed type is very useful for small work. Metric bits would be particularly useful because most helicopters use metric parts.

Sandpaper. A pack of assorted grades is essential.

Glue, including silicone, epoxy (the quick-set and the slow-set types) and CA, which dries in seconds.

Loctite, or a similar material, to prevent parts from vibrating loose. Get one bottle that is "removable" so the parts can be removed if required, and another made for high-temperature use around the engine and muffler. Although many helicopter kit instructions

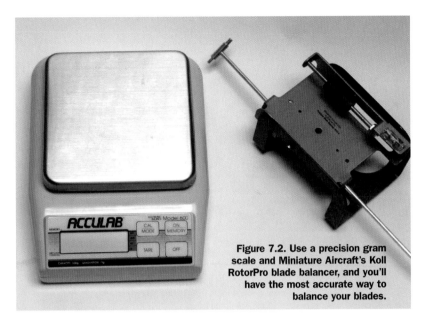

Figure 7.2. Use a precision gram scale and Miniature Aircraft's Koll RotorPro blade balancer, and you'll have the most accurate way to balance your blades.

suggest the use of the permanent type (which means that parts cannot be separated unless they're heated), I never use it.

Bearing grease and light oil. Small applicators with fine points are nice to place the oil and grease where needed on small parts. I also like the newer silicone oils, but almost any high-quality oil will do.

Wire cutters (one small and one medium).

Scissors.

Electrical tape (standard, but of good quality).

Rubber bands (medium to large from an office supply store).

Zip-ties in smaller sizes. These are handy to keep servo wires, receivers, batteries, etc., in place.

Soldering iron. I use a large one and a small 25W iron. You'll also need soldering paste, wire strippers, rosin-core solder, acid-core solder and, possibly, silver solder.

Toolbox to carry your gear to the flying field. I use the kind

designed for fishing tackle because of the many pull-out drawers and small compartments.

SPECIAL TOOLS
You might not have these in your shop, but you should buy them before you really need them. Don't run out of something special on a Saturday night when the stores are closed, and you have to wait until Monday to continue your work! Keep a small stock of the items most often needed.

Open-end wrenches. These come in packages containing various

sizes, standard or metric, but you'll need only the smallest.

Metric tap-and-die set. This isn't really a necessity, but I use mine often to make up the wire pieces I need (at a great savings compared with their usual cost). Generally, the 2mm and 3mm sizes are the most helpful, and they can be found in hardware stores.

Small (jewelers') screwdrivers. These are very small and usually come in a set of several sizes, both flat and cross-point.

Ball-link pliers. These are designed to pop the link off the ball for adjustments. You can use needle-nose pliers, but these special pliers make the job much easier, and you'll be amazed by how many times you'll use them in the shop and at the flying field.

Ball-link driver (similar to a hex driver, but this one is designed to hold a ball link).

Four-way wrench. This handy, cross-shaped tool has four nut drivers of different sizes at each point. The drivers are just right for glow plugs, prop nuts, etc. You could use the nut-driver set

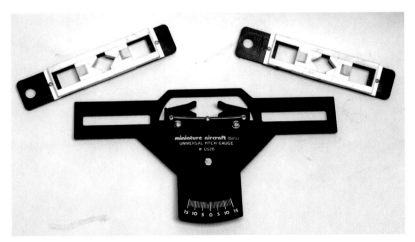

Figure 7.3. A pitch gauge is valuable in the workshop and at the flying field. It should be easy to align, should attach to rotor blades of any size and should be easy to read. The two paddle gauges are used for easy paddle alignment.

already mentioned for these tasks, but this wrench is so small and handy that I can't imagine not having one in my field box.

Double-stick tape. Commonly called servo tape, it has a foam center and adhesive on both sides. Available in a variety of thicknesses, the 1/16- and 1/8-inch thicknesses should work well for mounting part of the radio, etc., as described later.

Moto-tool. In the U.S., we usually refer to this tool by its brand name of Dremel, but I'm sure that other brands are available elsewhere. When this tool was first introduced to the hobby field many years ago, I didn't get one because I didn't think it would be of much use. After reading many articles about how useful it is, I bought one, and now I wouldn't trade it for any-thing. The Moto-Tool always has a way of making assembly and repairs easier and faster, and I rec-ommend the deluxe model with a variable speed control and a wide variety of bits and accessories.

Figure 7.4. You'll need a variety of glues, and petroleum jelly is an excellent lubricant for composite materials and rubber grommets.

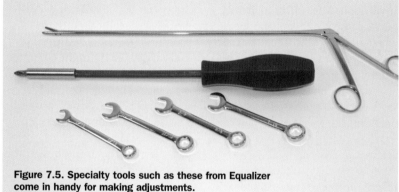

Figure 7.5. Specialty tools such as these from Equalizer come in handy for making adjustments.

WHERE & WHAT TO BUY

8

Where & What to Buy

By now, you have some idea about which helicopter and equipment you intend to buy, so where should you buy them? My aim in this short chapter isn't to tell you where to buy your equipment, but to help you with your choices.

BUYING ON THE WEB

Web prices are often very reasonable because these companies buy everything in quantity and at lower prices, and those savings are passed along to customers. Another advantage is quick service—quite important if you need a part, but the hobby shop is out of stock and may take several weeks to get it. With lower prices and speedy delivery, the Web has a lot to offer.

One disadvantage of buying online, however, may be the lack of advice and technical support. You must know exactly which products you want when you order. Not all Internet companies are this way; some were established by modelers who are very interested in customer satisfaction and are willing and able to advise you and stand behind their products. Just get to know the people you're dealing with.

LOCAL HOBBY SHOP

If you're lucky enough to live near a hobby shop whose staff is familiar with helicopters, see what they have to offer and of what assistance they may be as you learn to fly your heli. Here are a few of the advantages of a local hobby shop:

• You see the products before you buy them. When buying on the Web, you may have to know exactly what you want when you place the order. At a hobby shop, you can talk to someone who's knowledgeable and ask their advice. Seeing all the different brands will help you assess quality and value.

• Usually, dealers can give you advice on what local modelers use and why. Perhaps certain spare parts are more readily available or a particular item works best in your weather conditions. This advice can make quite a difference to your overall satisfaction with your eventual purchase.

• Your local dealer is also better able to stand behind the products he sells. Generally, if you have a problem with a particular product, the dealer will exchange it or return it to the manufacturer for repairs. For example, if your radio has a defective component, the only guarantee is from the radio manufacturer, and it might take weeks to have the repair made. In this case, it would be very convenient to have a local dealer who will get you airborne quickly. Because he deals with a limited number of customers, he is more apt to try harder to keep his customers satisfied. Also, at times, you might think a product is defective, but in reality, you just don't know how it works, and the dealer can show you how to use it properly.

• A local dealer who is knowledgeable about the products he sells can also be of great help during construction and when you're learning to fly. He has seen the mistakes made by other beginners, and he can help you to avoid making the same ones. He may also give lessons on how to set up the helicopter, how to hover, etc. If he doesn't do that himself, he may know someone who can help you.

• The dealer will also know which spare parts you might need in the future, and he'll probably have them in stock when you need them.

• No matter how much we like our helicopters, we always dream of the next one and how much better it will be. This is especially true if you have a model designed for beginners, and you plan to buy a more sophisticated one later on. When you want to sell the one you have, the dealer will help you. Most hobby shops have an assortment of models hanging from their ceilings—some for sale and ready to fly. You may be able to find just the right used helicopter to get you into the air at a reduced price, and the hobby dealer can start the helicopter and demonstrate its performance.

The main disadvantage of the local hobby shop is that it must charge higher prices than Internet stores because it just doesn't sell a sufficiently high volume. But when you consider its advantages, it may be in your best long-term interests to do business there and pay a little extra.

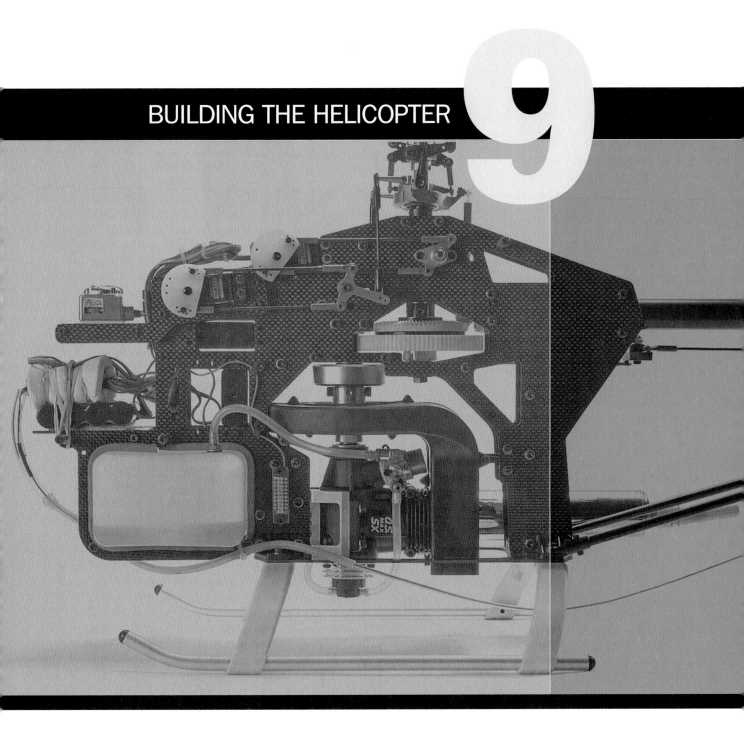

Building the Helicopter

Because helicopters vary, it's virtually impossible to supplement your kit's building instructions by giving you details of building techniques that apply to all of them. There are many construction techniques and many pitfalls to watch out for, and I discuss them in this chapter.

Helicopter instructions sometime assume that you have experience in building helicopters and may therefore not provide the details that novices need. For those of you who are experienced, I present alternative techniques that may be helpful.

The guidelines presented here are for a typical pod-and-boom helicopter, i.e., a helicopter without a scale fuselage. Most scale helicopters are the same as the basic pod-and-boom machines, but they've been cosmetically enhanced with a fuselage to give an overall scale effect

One of the first things you'll notice about your helicopter kit is how carefully it has been packaged to protect the delicate parts. Whenever I open a new kit, I have an urge to take out all the components for a closer inspection. There are two reasons, however, why you should resist this impulse. First, everything has been packaged in a very efficient way, and you may not be able to get everything back into the box, thereby leaving some components out in the open where they could be misplaced, damaged, or even lost. Second, the parts are packaged in many individual plastic

Figure 9-1. Balancing the flybar on a Du-Bro balancer. Note the wheel collars that have been added to the flybar to adjust balance.

bags to keep all the smaller parts separated, so they may be opened to coincide with steps in the building instructions. Because many of these parts are metal, it's rather easy for them to wear through their packaging during shipping, and by taking them out of the box, you could lose some of the smaller components. Of course, you won't know they have been misplaced until you need them, so until you need them, resist the temptation to take the parts out of the box.

The first time you assemble a helicopter kit, it's also a little unnerving to see all those small components, so look closely at the instruction manual and at any

"blow-up" views. Although you don't need to read the instructions completely to see where each screw goes, it's a good idea to get an idea of the big picture, i.e., how the components are assembled and how they, in turn, fit together to make a whole helicopter. Because the helicopter is unique, the names of its components will probably be new to you, and a look at the instructions will give you an opportunity to become familiar with some of the terminology you will use later.

One other point should be kept in the forefront as you build and fly, and that's the need for safety. A model helicopter can be a great deal of fun but only if it's assembled and maintained properly and flown safely. Because of the tremendous power of electric motors and model engines and the energy potential of the main and tail rotors, an accident could be disastrous for you or a spectator. Therefore, take your time and assemble the helicopter exactly according to the instruction manual, and when it's completed, operate it very carefully.

GENERAL BUILDING GUIDELINES

Although you'll probably be keen to start construction, you'll also find the building quite tiring—at least, mentally. You'll learn a lot about helicopters as you build, and going from the instructions to the blow-up diagrams and then to the helicopter itself requires a lot of concentration. Work only when you feel like it, and don't push yourself to finish a certain section before you rest for the night. When you're tired and hurried, you'll make mistakes.

Before you start, prepare your work area so you won't have to look for tools later that you should have had on hand. Take a closer look at the first section of the instruction manual and the blow-ups, closely review the first few building steps, and make sure that you have the tools necessary to

complete them. Have a clean, well-lit surface to work on, and keep a muffin tin or some other tray with many compartments nearby to hold all the small parts when you've opened a particular bag.

Follow these guidelines as they apply to your particular helicopter. As you go through the instructions, check off each step, or paragraph, as you complete it. Then, when you take a break, it will be obvious where you left off, and you won't miss a small but vital step in the building process.

Certain parts have to be lubricated when they're assembled because they'll be inaccessible later. Your instructions should tell you the sort of lubrication to use; it may even be supplied. If no other guidance is provided, use a good-quality bearing grease for open bearings: press the grease into the bearings to fill all the space. For other sliding surfaces, use a good-quality oil. For longer-lasting protection, I prefer oils that include silicone.

Many of the nuts in the kit will have self-locking inserts to prevent them from vibrating loose. On any screw that doesn't use this type of nut, you must use a drop or two of Loctite, or its equivalent, to prevent that screw from loosening during a flight. Because

of the high number of moving parts in a helicopter, there's always some vibration, and without Loctite, the screws will usually loosen with time. Before you apply the Loctite, however, clean the threads of the screws (preferably with a solvent such as lacquer thinner) to remove any oil or preservative that could interfere with the bonding of the Loctite.

There are different types of Loctite. The blue Loctite does an excellent job, and it allows disassembly when necessary for maintenance and repairs. The red Loctite is designed for permanent applications, and it shouldn't be used unless it's specifically called for. It makes joined fasteners very difficult to disassemble, but the heat from a match or a soldering gun will help to break the bond if you have to.

Take care when installing small screws, nuts and bolts. Although they're strong and designed to take the stresses of the helicopter, they're easy to over-tighten and strip their threads. This is especially a problem when you tighten small setscrews with a hex wrench. Too much torque will cause the wrench to slip and round the setscrew's hex, and that will make it very difficult to remove the screw. All screws and bolts should be tightened using

Figure 9-2. All the parts on the tail rotor must move freely; lubricate them with a light oil.

Figure 9-3. The Venture 50 frame and head are strong and light and made mostly of composite materials.

Figure 9-4. The Venture 50 side frames are like a clamshell for maximum strength. Check their alignment and freedom of movement before you tighten the screws.

Figure 9-5. A direct servo connection to the CCPM swashplate. Note the wrap on the servo leads.

only moderate pressure.

As you progress through the assembly, you'll encounter parts that are meant to slide or rotate, and these must be checked to ensure maximum freedom of movement without slop.

These parts include:
• The flybar and its connections to the rotor head. No lateral movement in the flybar should be possible, but it should rotate freely as well as tilt up and down.
• The collective mechanism should operate freely, without any slop, throughout its entire range.
• The main gear should be able to rotate freely in one direction (assuming you have an autorotation clutch).
• All the pushrods should operate their helicopter functions freely but without slop in the controls. Push and pull on the pushrods to check for freedom of movement during assembly.
• A clevis is a plastic device that's screwed onto the end of a pushrod and used to attach the pushrod either to a servo or to a bellcrank. The clevis can be opened so that the small pin can be placed into the servo-wheel hole, etc., but care must be taken to ensure a correct fit. If the hole in the servo wheel or arm is too small, it could cause the pin to wear or break. If the hole is too large, there will be slop in the

linkage. Once it's in position, use a small piece of rubber tubing as a rubber band, and stretch it around the clevis to lock it closed.
• A ball link is similar to a clevis, but a ball is mounted on the servo or bellcrank, and the link is snapped onto the ball. A ball link is generally preferable to a clevis, especially in areas of high loads, because a ball link is stronger and slop-free. New links can, however, have a very tight fit to the ball, and this can cause binding between the two. An easy solution is to apply a little petroleum jelly to the ball; it will then wear in and fit properly after a few flights. Also, the ball link may not be symmetrical—one side may be designed to snap onto the ball. Check your instructions or, if the link has any markings, place the side with the markings on the outside of the ball connection.

As you assemble the helicopter, take time to make sure that everything looks and feels right. If it doesn't look right, it probably isn't. If it feels too stiff, binds at the extremes, feels sloppy, etc., it must be corrected right away.

After you've assembled the heli (or when directed by your building instructions), lightly coat all of its moving metal parts with oil. Many helicopters use a lot of glass-filled nylon or plastic parts to reduce weight, and if they aren't

CNC-machined, they may require a certain "wear-in" to operate freely. Don't be too concerned if they seem a little stiff when first assembled; they should free up after a tank or two of fuel. A little petroleum jelly on the nylon moving parts will act as a lubricant, but be careful not to overdo it, or the excess will attract dirt.

Parts should be balanced as required during assembly. For example: before you mount the tail-rotor hub and blades on the tail-rotor output shaft, balance the entire unit to prevent vibration. It's a lot easier to do the balancing during assembly rather than find out later that something is vibrating because isolating the source can be difficult and will probably require disassembly.

CONSTRUCTION
Let me caution you not to redesign the helicopter during construction. There are times when you may think a part should be changed or redesigned, but chances are, the manufacturer has already considered the change and found the original design better. The only area where I would make a small but significant change is to grind a flat spot on a shaft for a setscrew, if there isn't a flat already there.

Your helicopter kit should contain many bags of parts, each to be used for a specific area of assembly. Open only one bag at a time—when called for in the instructions—and put the parts in a suitable partitioned container such as an egg carton or a muffin tin. This will allow you to separate the parts as needed, see all the small parts and keep them in a secure place. Also, before you open a parts bag, make sure that you have the time to complete that phase of construction. If you were to stop assembly at some midpoint, it would be easy to have a mishap and lose some of the remaining parts.

MAIN FRAME

This is the area usually discussed first in the instruction manual, and care must be taken to make sure that the sides are aligned properly because they will hold everything else. To be sure they're aligned, insert all the screws, but tighten them only loosely, and then stand the structure on the table. Both sides should be aligned and standing vertically. Remember to lubricate the control levers and other subassemblies when they're added to the main frame, or they may be difficult to reach after construction has been completed.

The helicopter's landing skids are often a problem because vibration may cause the front skid tips to turn in flight, and that could cause them to trip on something while landing. You can easily prevent this by drilling a small hole through the skid mount and skid to accept a small sheet-metal screw. If the hole is drilled from the inside of the skid, no one will even know it's there.

ENGINE, CLUTCH & STARTER SHAFT

Most helicopters use a fan mounted on the engine in place of the propeller to constantly blow cooling air over the engine.

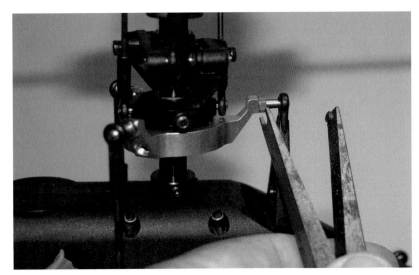

Figure 9-6. Special ball-link pliers protect the ball link and facilitate adjustments.

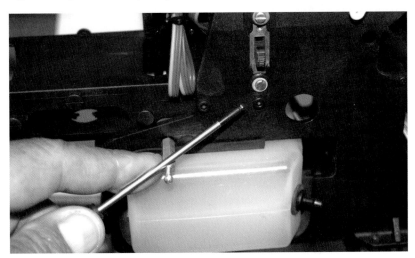

Figure 9-7. Hardened metric drivers make building a pleasure.

The fan turns at high rpm, and if it's out of balance, it will be noticeable throughout the helicopter. Therefore, it should be balanced during construction. A High Point balancer is a very useful addition to your workshop, and you can use it to balance the cooling fan. Generally, sanding the fins on the heavy side of the fan should be all that's needed to get it just right.

Because of its small size, the fan is hard to hold while tightening the prop nut. One method to tighten the nut is to wedge something into the exhaust to prevent the piston from moving. This is almost a sure way to ruin the engine because a great strain is placed on the connecting rod, which is not designed to take this amount of force. Instead, remove the carburetor and place a wooden dowel between the crankshaft and the engine case to prevent the crankshaft from moving. After putting Loctite on the threads, tighten the fan in place with moderate pressure.

When the fan has been mounted, make sure that it runs true; this is best accomplished with a dial indicator. This instrument is inexpensive, and it's usually available at hardware stores, Sears, etc. It measures movements as small as 0.001 inch;

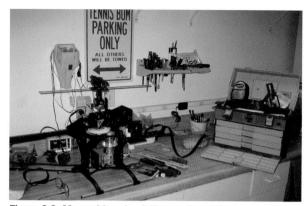

Figure 9-8. My workbench; all the most used tools are within easy reach.

Figure 9-9. The Miniature Aircraft X-Cell Fury's composite side frame. Follow the instructions, and check the alignment of all the parts.

when the dial isn't moving, the object is running perfectly true.

Mount the engine in a workshop vise with the dial indicator touching the outside of the fan hub. With the engine glow plug removed, the engine can be turned over fairly easily, and the dial indicator will reveal any wobble in the fan hub. If there's any wobble over 0.001 inch, loosen the fan, rotate it slightly, and then retighten it. If the fan hub and engine were machined correctly, there should be perfect run-out, but a slight adjustment of the fan may be necessary.

Gently put the engine into position inside the main frame, and slightly tighten the engine-mounting screws. If the engine is not pushed completely into the clutch-bell housing, the clutch will not completely engage. However, if the engine is pushed too tightly into the clutch-bell housing, the clutch will not turn freely. Experiment by moving the engine slightly in the side frames to get it as high as possible without binding the clutch.

MAIN GEAR

The mesh of the clutch pinion gear with the main gear is very important because too tight a fit will cause the gears to bind and put a load on the entire drive system. If the gear mesh is too loose,

however, the gears will bang back and forth as power is added and reduced, and this will cause the gears to wear quickly and even to strip the main gear.

Some helicopters have CNC-machined side frames and main gear that are made to such high tolerances that no adjustment is provided. If your helicopter does allow a gear-mesh adjustment, most instructions I've seen recommend that you adjust the gear mesh until a piece of paper will just fit between the two gears. Another technique I've used successfully is to gently turn the main gear. Any out-of-round condition in the gear will show up as a tight spot in the gear mesh, and at this point, the mesh should be adjusted. Hold the clutch-bell housing in one hand, and then rock the main gear back and forth. If the mesh is set correctly, there will be very little play. If it's possible to reduce the play, continue doing so until you reach a point where there's just the slightest play. The main gear should now turn freely, with no tight spots or wobbling.

HEAD ASSEMBLY

The head, swashplate and washout unit contain many small parts that must be assembled with the greatest care if you're to have a smooth, vibration-free helicop-

ter. During this assembly, many screws, balls, bearings, etc., will be mounted on small individual parts, so take a good look at the pictures and diagrams provided to get an overall feel for the many parts you will be assembling. I have found it best to first mount the smallest pieces, such as balls and setscrews, on individual parts prior to assembly. Again, use Loctite where needed, and don't over-tighten.

After assembling the rotor head's basic structure, check that all the parts are slop-free and have complete freedom of movement. A Robart High Point balancer, or a similar one, can then be used to check the balance between the two blade grips. Attach the completed head to the main shaft, minus the rotor blades and flybar, and then place the main shaft on the balancer. If the head is out of balance, place a small washer or two on the blade-attaching bolt of the light blade holder to bring it into balance.

Properly mounting the flybar and paddles on the head is critical to the helicopter's overall performance and balance, but most of the instructions I've seen are rather vague on this step. Although it isn't particularly hard, the instructions should be followed very carefully to be sure that proper alignment and balance are achieved.

The first objective is to ensure that the flybar is exactly centered on the head. To do this, slide the flybar into position and use a ruler to measure the distance from the side of the head to each tip of the flybar. If measuring from a point on the head isn't practical, measure from each control arm or flybar weight, as long as they're the same on each side of the head. By looking at your particular helicopter, you should be able to find a measuring point that will allow you to center the flybar. Once it's centered, mount the remaining pieces on the flybar. I also mount a wheel collar on each side of the flybar to use later for balancing (wheel collars are available at your hobby store).

Next, mount the paddles on the flybar. They must also be equidistant from the head, so measure the distance from some point on the head to each paddle. One paddle will probably have to be screwed in or out slightly, and even then, they probably won't be exactly the same distance from the head. Get them as close as you can, and align the paddles to their rough position for now.

Now you're ready to balance the flybar by slipping the main shaft onto the head and placing it on a High Point (or similar) balancer. If the flybar is perfectly centered and the other components are equidistant from the head and weigh the same, then the head will be in perfect balance. However, this very seldom happens, and it's why I use wheel collars for slight balance adjustments. With the flybar in the horizontal position, position the wheel collars as needed to bring the flybar into balance.

With the head and flybar balanced, the last step is to adjust the control arms and paddles to their proper positions. Flybar paddle gauges can be used to set up the paddles to their proper and aligned positions. Your instructions should provide other specific setup parameters for your particular helicopter.

TAIL-ROTOR DRIVE

Helicopters are getting away from having a wire-driven tail rotor, but if yours has one, there is a "gotcha." The tail-rotor drive unit, which turns the drive wire, must be pointing directly down the tail boom. As you can imagine, if it isn't, the wire will whip around, and this will not only cause vibration, but it will also cause the wire to break at the drive unit.

To check this during assembly, simply see whether it looks right. The accuracy of our eyes is amazing, and just by looking from the rear of the helicopter (before the tail boom has been installed), we'll see the tail-rotor drive unit pointing to the center of the tail-boom supports. If there's still any doubt or you'd like to go a step further, simply install a small piece of extra wire in the drive unit, pointing the wire directly between the tail-boom supports.

The other concern is with the mesh of the tail-rotor drive gear and the main gear. Most main gears are also used to drive the tail rotor, so the gear mesh here is also important. However, because the tail-rotor drive gear is usually rather fine, I try to mesh it as tightly as I can without placing noticeable drag on the system. But this requires that you do two things at once: set the mesh of the drive gear and make sure that the drive unit is pointing in the proper direction.

When you think you have it right, spin the main gear. The entire drive system should turn freely. Some main gears also require a little breaking in, so after your first day's flying, check for proper gear mesh.

An upgrade to the wire-driven tail rotor is the tube drive. This system is similar to the wire-driven tail, but a hollow tube is used in place of the wire. This tube can be made of a light metal or, more commonly, fiberglass, and it has the advantage of being completely free of flex.

Possibly the most common type of tail-rotor drive is the belt-drive system. Here, the wire or tube is replaced with a toothed belt that is connected between the tail rotor and a pinion gear that runs off the main gear. The belt-drive system is less costly to design and produce because it's

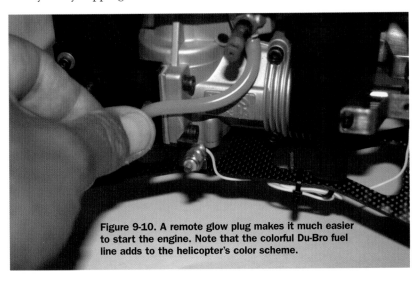

Figure 9-10. A remote glow plug makes it much easier to start the engine. Note that the colorful Du-Bro fuel line adds to the helicopter's color scheme.

very simple, and it does away with the gears and some bearings used in the wire and tube drives. The only words of caution with a belt drive are that you should ensure that the belt tension is as specified in the instructions for a smooth operation with a minimum of drag.

TAIL ROTOR & GEARBOX

Most tail-rotor gearboxes are rather straightforward in construction, but because of their very high rpm and our inability to get inside when construction is complete, it's very important to do the job correctly the first time. This means that not only should the gears mesh properly, but their positions should also be marked on the shafts and a flat filed (if not already filed by the manufacturer) to accept the setscrew. This flat is easily made with the help of a Moto-Tool and a grinding disc.

Again, Loctite must be used to keep the setscrews in place; I first put a drop in the hole and then another drop on the setscrew, so the Loctite will fill any spaces between the gear, the setscrew and the shaft. Be careful not to overtighten the setscrew because it can be stripped fairly easily, and it will have to be removed and replaced before the Loctite dries, or it will be even more difficult to remove later.

Some tail-rotor gearboxes make a provision for lubrication after completion; others do not. If yours must be lubricated during construction, do so while you can still get to the gears and bearings. Use a good-quality bearing grease and fill as much of the space as possible. I've never known it to be harmful to put as much grease as you can into the gearbox, but having too little can quickly result in a lot of damage.

The tail-rotor blades also have to be balanced, and the easiest

way to do this is to mount the blades on their center hub and then mount the whole system on a High Point balancer. The blades can be balanced either by lightly sanding the underside of the heavier blade, or by adding a small strip of blade-covering material to the light blade.

The tightness of the tail-rotor blades in their blade grips is critical to having a smoothly running tail-rotor system. If the blades are too loose, they will move excessively as they change pitch in flight, and if they are too tight, they may not extend to their normal flight position. Either case will result in a high-frequency tail-rotor vibration. Therefore, as you tighten the tail-rotor blade's mounting bolts, move the blades back and forth so they both have the same amount of drag. The blades should be able to move, but they should not be loose enough to drop under their own weight.

TAIL BOOM & FINS

Mounting the tail boom on the main frames and connecting the tail-rotor unit is usually easy. I haven't had many problems with the tail-rotor unit, but I've had problems with the tail boom's coming loose from the main frame. To be sure that the tail boom doesn't slip out of its position on the main frame, drill a small hole through a side of the main frame and into the tail boom. Then insert a small sheet-metal screw, but make sure that it's not so long that it interferes with the tail-rotor drive system. This simple "five-cent" technique could have saved one of my helicopters.

The horizontal fin affects only the flying characteristics of the helicopter during fast forward flight, and even then, the only real difference I've ever noticed was that a larger horizontal fin

increased the diameter of the loops. To put it another way: the larger horizontal fin reduced the effectiveness of the elevator control. Many of my helicopters don't even have a horizontal fin, and I haven't noticed any appreciable difference between their flight characteristics and those of others.

The vertical fin, however, is quite a different story. As already mentioned, the vertical fin adds greatly to the helicopter's yaw stability, even in a hover with a slight wind. If you are not going to use a heading-hold gyro, you may want to increase the size of the vertical fin supplied with your helicopter. Most helicopter designs are a compromise between flight stability for novices and aerobatic maneuverability for more advanced fliers. To reduce the yaw movements while you learn to hover, it would be better to have a rather large vertical fin for an increased "weathervane" effect. The vertical fin does much the same job as the feathers on an arrow: it keeps the "pointy end going first." The design of the fin isn't important, and a general guide would be to increase its size to about twice that recommended by the manufacturer. Also, to protect the tail rotor while you learn to hover, make this fin long enough to extend below the tail rotor by about 2 inches. Generally, the fin can be made out of light, $3/32$- to $3/16$-inch plywood; remember to paint the wood with a fuelproof paint to protect it from the engine exhaust.

FUEL TANK

Each helicopter design calls for a specific method of mounting the fuel tank, but if you can, it's best to mount the tank using foam rubber to reduce the fuel foaming that can be caused by minor vibration. The pick-up tube inside the fuel tank should also have a weight, or

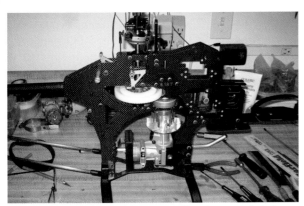

Figure 9-11. Work slowly and check off each completed step on the instructions. Stop working when you're tired, or you'll risk making mistakes.

Figure 9-12. Bend a coat-hanger wire as required to hold the helicopter by its flybar, and attach it to the garage or basement ceiling. It keeps your model out of harm's way and prevents it from developing hangar rash.

"clunk," to keep the pick-up at the bottom of the tank so it gets all the fuel. When the tank has been installed, turn the helicopter to make sure that the clunk is free to move inside the tank.

Some like to mount a fuel filter in the fuel line between the tank and the engine. I don't disagree with this technique, but since I've had more problems with the filter than with dirt in the fuel, I don't use one. Instead, I double-filter my fuel before it ever gets to the tank, and this keeps the fuel clean.

One final point about the fuel tank: if at all possible, pressurize the tank with muffler pressure to help feed fuel to the engine. My tank usually has three fittings: one to feed the engine, one to refuel and one to accept muffler pressure. I cap the refuel fitting with a piece of fuel tubing and a small screw, which is removed during refueling. This makes a "closed" system to use the muffler pressure.

Some like to use a header tank between the main fuel tank and the engine. This header tank is usually a 1- or 2-ounce fuel tank that has the following advantages: it provides a little extra fuel; if the main fuel tank is hard to see, it makes it easier to see when you're low on fuel; and it eliminates air bubbles coming from a foaming main fuel tank. However, many also believe that a header tank provides a steady flow of fuel to the engine, but that isn't the case. The engine views a header tank as nothing more than a wide spot in the fuel line, and the flow of fuel to the engine is determined by muffler pressure and the difference in height from the level of fuel (usually in the main tank) to the carburetor.

ROTOR BLADES

If rotor blades are not provided with your kit, they will have to be purchased separately. Available in a variety of materials, including wood, fiberglass, plastic and carbon fiber, some are ready to fly while others require finishing and balancing. Whichever blades you decide to use, always check their spanwise CG and overall balance before flying with them. Although there are many techniques to balance rotor blades, they all require at least two of the following because if you have any two, the third is automatically guaranteed:
• Matching spanwise CG (and, possibly, chordwise).
• Matching the overall weight of the blades.
• Bringing the two blades into overall balance on a High Point (or similar) balancer.

For further explanation on the theory of rotor-blade balancing, refer to Chapter 12, "Helicopter Theory and Control."

Techniques for balancing rotor blades range from simple, inexpensive methods to complicated, costly measurements obtained using delicate balances and scales. It is important to obtain the best possible rotor-blade balance because balanced blades offer the best flight performance with the least vibration. The variety of balancing techniques, therefore, provides options; your choice will depend on the degree of accuracy you want compared with the time and cost involved for expensive equipment. And because this is a book on basics, I'll first present a quick and easy technique that will produce adequately accurate results, and then I'll describe what I think is the most accurate and most costly method to date.

BLADE BALANCING— THE INEXPENSIVE WAY

First, on a flat table, find the spanwise CG by rolling each blade on a round pencil. Make sure the pencil is at a 90-degree angle to the rotor blade, and mark the balance point of each blade on its leading edge. Then hold the blades together, and their CG marks should line up. If they don't, mark each blade to indicate which way its CG must be moved. Wrap a piece of blade-covering material or electrical tape around the blade, either near the tip or root as required to move the CG in the proper direction. I actually prefer electrical tape because it's inexpensive, it's readily available in my workshop, it sticks well but can be removed easily when needed and it's fairly heavy, so you usually need only a little. After adding the weight, recheck the blade CG and repeat as often as is necessary until the two blades match.

The final step is to bring the blades into overall balance using a blade balancer. Mount the blades on the balancer, and check their balance. Wrap electrical tape around the light blade at its CG point until the blades balance. Blades are ready to fly when they're level and their CGs match.

As you become proficient at balancing rotor blades, you might want to combine the two steps of matching CGs and overall balance. To do this, use the balancer first to determine which is the light blade, and then add weight to that blade until its CG matches that of the other blade. It takes a little trial and error to obtain overall balance, but it should reduce the amount of tape required.

BLADE BALANCING— THE EXPENSIVE WAY

You can match the spanwise and chordwise CG of the blades more accurately by using the Koll RotorPro balancer, available from Miniature Aircraft. I rarely recommend one product over another, but this is probably the most significant advance in blade balancing since Robart introduced its High Point balancer.

A further balancing refinement would be to use a gram scale to weigh each blade. By doing that, you can very accurately match the blades' CGs and guarantee that they both weigh the same, and you have the most accurately balanced set of blades yet available.

Whichever method you use to balance your blades, it's important to remember that we're still working in a static environment rather than a dynamic moving environment. Many years ago, automobile tires were balanced on a bubble balancer, but no matter how good a job we did, they always seemed to be out of balance at some speed. Now the bubble balancer has been replaced by the dynamic balancer: the wheel is placed in a machine and spun at a high rate. The machine indicates how much weight to use and where to add it to provide a wheel that will be perfectly balanced at any speed. This is exactly the kind of machine we need for our entire rotor system. Unfortunately, as far as I know, no one has designed such a machine, but that doesn't mean it can't be done. Once such a dynamic balancing machine has been perfected, we'll be able to dramatically improve our helicopters' performance.

BLADE VISIBILITY

As the rotor blades turn in flight, we need to be able to discern two things:
• First, we need to be able to distinguish one blade tip from the other to check blade tracking. Two pieces of tape of different colors are usually provided—one for each blade tip. (I discuss this in a later chapter on blade tracking.)
• Second, it would also be nice to see the entire rotor disc in flight to aid in orientation and control of the helicopter. For a larger heli, I cut four, 2-inch (approximately) strips of blade covering material or shelf covering in a color that contrasts with the rotor blade. I put one strip on the top of a rotor blade near its tip and trim it flush

with the blade's trailing edge. I cut the other end just long enough to wrap slightly around the leading edge to prevent the oncoming air from getting underneath it. In a similar manner, I put another strip of covering 3 or 4 inches away from the first, and then I cover the second rotor blade as I did the first. When the blades rotate, the strips will show up as a two bull's-eyes, but only on the top, since the bottoms of the blades aren't covered.

Now stand back and look at your helicopter. You should not only feel proud of what you have accomplished, but you should also check to see whether everything looks right. The most common problem I see with new helicopters concerns the main and tail rotors: the linkages aren't correctly installed, the rotor blades are on backwards, or some other obvious correction needs to be made. Remember: if it doesn't look right, it probably isn't.

HOW TO HANDLE YOUR HELICOPTER

When handling your helicopter, take care to avoid damaging the pushrods, links, servos, etc. When you lift it, do so by holding one or both blade grips. They're designed to hold many times the weight of the helicopter, and this approach will keep your hand well away from the pushrods that go to the rotor head. When you carry your helicopter, hold one blade grip, and walk with the tail boom facing forward. By doing it this way, you'll see the tail boom and be able to guide it around objects.

Rotor blades can also be folded back and supported along the tail boom for ease of storage and transportation. Keep unnecessary pressure off the pushrods and servos, and support the weight of the blades when you fold them back along the tail boom.

RADIO INSTALLATION

Radio Installation

I n this chapter, we'll install the servos, the receiver, the airborne battery, the switch harness and the gyro, and we'll connect the radio equipment to the helicopter's controls. We'll make further control refinements later, when we start the engine and the helicopter is "trimmed out" for the first time.

If you haven't already done so, charge the transmitter and receiver batteries overnight (according to the manufacturer's instructions) because installing the radio requires that you operate the servos while making a lot of adjustments.

With your radio on your workbench, connect all the radio equipment according to the instructions; turn on the transmitter first and then the airborne switch. Center the trims on the transmitter, and make sure that all of the servos have their output arm or wheel at 90 degrees to the length of the servo. If a servo arm isn't at 90 degrees to the servo, remove the arm and rotate it slightly until it's in the right position. Some servos have numbered output arms, and each arm is at a slightly different angle to the servo. A splined output shaft on the servo makes it easy to do this job accurately.

You should also check your radio's instruction manual to see whether you can make other adjustments to your specific servo. In particular, check all the throws at 100 percent, and inhibit the idle-up, throttle-hold and revolution-mixing functions. You won't

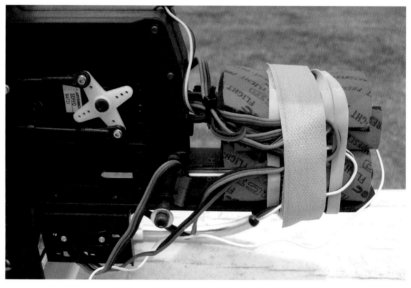

Figure 10-1. The receiver and battery pack are wrapped in protective foam and secured to the helicopter. I use a combination of rubber bands and hook-and-loop strips to keep things secure for 3D flying.

use these functions during your initial hover attempts, but you'll add them later as needed.

Next, make sure that everything is working properly. As the control sticks are moved through their range of travel, the servos should move smoothly and quickly and should follow the control-stick movements. Also, range-check the radio completely before you install it in a helicopter. Any range degradation after installation will probably be due to the radio installation itself, and it will have to be corrected.

Range-checking procedures for radios vary slightly. Check your instructions to see how far the transmitter antenna should be extended, if at all, and what a satisfactory operating range is under these conditions. The receiver and its associated components can be

left in the manufacturer's carton, completely connected, and the receiver antenna can be extended to its full length and left hanging from the carton. For this range check, don't put the radio on anything metallic, as this might cause signal reflectance, which could adversely affect the radio's range. Ask a friend to hold the carton at about waist height—high enough to avoid having the receiver antenna dragging on the ground—turn everything on, and make sure that the radio is functioning properly.

Collapse the transmitter antenna to the length specified in your radio instructions, and walk away from it slowly while operating the controls. All the servos should move smoothly and rapidly to match your control commands. Eventually, you'll

Figure 10-2. Note the push-pull controls on the Fry for strength and precision and that all the servo wires have been tucked neatly away.

Figure 10-3. The Freya has an external servo-output-shaft support for extreme 3D flying.

reach a distance at which the servo operation is erratic. Now, one step at a time, move back until full control is again established. This distance to the receiver is your effective range check; compare it with that recommended in your instructions. If you can't get the minimum range-check distance for your radio, check the following:
• Are the batteries for the receiver and the transmitter both fully charged? If they aren't, charge them fully and do the range check again.
• Does the meter on the transmitter show that it's transmitting a signal? If it does, does it deflect to the proper operating range with the transmitter antenna fully extended? If the needle doesn't show the correct operation, perhaps the transmitter battery isn't fully charged. Charge it again, according to your instruction manual, just to be sure. If your transmitter has a frequency module, first turn the transmitter power switch off, and then check to verify that the module has been properly installed. Again, turn the power switch on and

check for proper operation. If you still can't get the proper meter deflection, send the radio to a repair facility to be checked.

When you do the range check, make sure that the receiver antenna isn't close to the servos or battery, etc., as this might affect the range.

If your range check isn't satisfactory, your radio isn't working correctly, and the cause must be determined. You may have to return the entire system (including the charger) to the manufacturer or a designated repair facility.

SERVO MOUNTING
Make sure that the transmitter and receiver are both turned off, and then disconnect the servos and the battery from the receiver. Using the rubber mounting grommets, metal eyelets and self-tapping screws supplied with your radio, mount the aileron servo in its proper location. Ensure that only the rubber mounting grommets touch the structure. Tighten the mounting screws until the rubber grommets are slightly compressed. If you

tighten the screws too much, the rubber grommets will be compressed so much that they can't act as shock absorbers. If they aren't tightened enough, the servo might vibrate in its mounts. The mounting screws are tight enough when the servo is secure, and the rubber grommets aren't fully compressed. Mount the other servos in a similar manner.

Your servos should come with a round servo wheel and other servo arms. For training purposes, the servo wheel will be used on the aileron, elevator and collective servos, and an output with an extended arm will be needed for the rudder and throttle servos. Verify that the servo wheel/arm is at 90 degrees to the servo body with the radio turned on and that the transmitter sticks and trims are in the neutral position. You may have to recheck the center position of the servos as they're set up, because the output arms/wheels are easily moved off-center when the radio is off.

Most helicopter kits supply the proper balls to mount on the servo, but you can buy them separately if you have to. Mount the

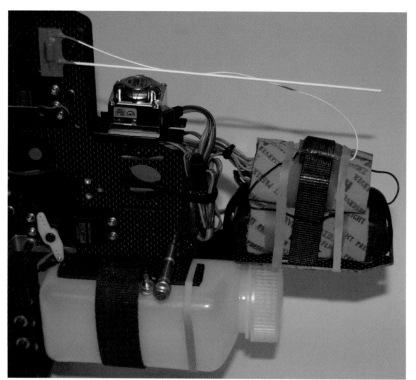

Figure 10-4. A base-loaded whip antenna (straight white wire at the top) makes a neat installation. All the wires are zip-tied for neatness. Note the rubber band around the fuel tank to keep it securely on the frame.

ball links on the inner holes of only the aileron, elevator and collective servos. This should provide the initial pushrod throw requirements as described in more detail in Chapter 11. Also, if there is room to use an extra nut as a spacer between the ball and the servo arm, it will make it easier to remove the ball link for an adjustment.

The helicopter kit also contains the required pushrods cut to the proper length. Starting with the aileron servo, screw the ball link onto both ends of the proper pushrod, as shown in your instructions. When the pushrod is connected to the servo, adjust the pushrod's length so that the swashplate is level when viewed right to left on the helicopter. If your helicopter is supplied with snap-on clevises, to make sure that they don't come open in flight, cut an ⅛-inch piece of fuel tubing and put it around the cle-

vis to lock it closed.

As a final check of the aileron control system, disconnect the pushrod from the servo, move the pushrod back and forth as the servo would, and make sure that the swashplate moves right and left without binding or rubbing. One common cause of binding in a control system is that a ball link is too tightly connected to the ball. This can be corrected by loosening the mounting bolt by ⅛ turn and allowing the ball to rotate on the bolt.

If your helicopter has clockwise-rotating main rotor blades (viewed from above), you'll have to trim the swashplate slightly to the right to counter the torque and tail rotor. To do this, turn one aileron clevis two complete turns on the pushrod (in or out, as required) to give the swashplate the slightest tilt to the right when the servo is in its neutral position.

In a similar way, make up the

elevator pushrod and adjust it to very slightly tilt the swashplate forwards toward the nose of the helicopter. This isn't needed to counter torque, but it's used as a learning technique that I'll describe later. Adjust the collective servo pushrod so that the collective range is at its midpoint when the servo-wheel ball link is at 90 degrees to the servo body.

For slightly greater throw, the ball link on the rudder servo should be positioned on the second hole out from the center on the servo arm. Connect the tail-rotor pushrod to the servo so that the tail-rotor bellcrank is in its midpoint position when the rudder servo is at neutral. For the moment, don't be concerned about adjusting the tail-rotor blades.

Remove the throttle-servo output arm. It's a little more difficult to adjust the pushrod between the servo and the engine carburetor than it was to adjust the control functions you've worked with so far because the throw required by the carburetor must be matched to the throw of the throttle servo. It's also advantageous to have the throttle open sooner than the collective so that the engine will have the power to support the rotor speed needed by the main rotor blades. If the throttle opens too late, the engine will be bogged down by the drag of the blades, and it will never be able to get up to proper operating speed. This can cause the engine to overheat and quit, and you might even ruin your engine.

To make sure that the throttle opens enough before the collective is increased, the throttle-output arm should be mounted as shown in Figure 10-5 when it's in the idle position. Note that the throttle is opened when the servo arm rotates to the right, and the initial servo movement produces a large pushrod movement. Near the full-power position (Figure 10-6), any servo movement produces very little movement in the throttle pushrod. This arrangement gives an early opening to the throttle for the power required.

The other requirement of the throttle servo is that it must completely stop the engine when required, and this is accomplished with the throttle-trim function on the transmitter. The throttle pushrod will be adjusted to completely close the throttle when the transmitter throttle stick is in the full idle position and the idle trim is in the full idle position. Therefore, as the throttle trim is advanced, the carburetor will open slightly and allow you to adjust the idle speed.

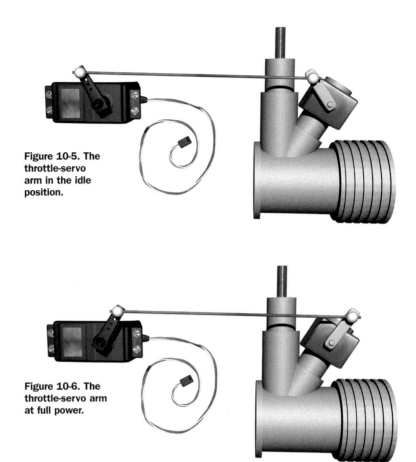

Figure 10-5. The throttle-servo arm in the idle position.

Figure 10-6. The throttle-servo arm at full power.

Throttle servo connection & setup

1. Connect only the throttle servo and the battery to the receiver; turn on the transmitter and receiver and check for proper servo operation.

2. Bring the throttle stick and throttle trim on the transmitter to the full idle (aft or down) position.

3. If you haven't already done so, mount the ball link in the middle hole of the servo-output arm.

4. Attach the servo arm so it's a little past 90 degrees, or slightly away from the engine.

5. Adjust the pushrod length so that the carburetor will be completely closed against its stop when the throttle servo is fully closed.

6. Connect the pushrod only to the throttle-output arm—not to the throttle-servo arm—and move the throttle stick on the transmitter to the full-throttle position.

7. With your hand, move the carburetor arm to its full open position; if you're lucky, the clevis will line up properly with the ball link. If it doesn't line up properly, the servo will either try to overdrive the throttle or it won't open the carburetor completely.

8. Check your radio's instruction manual for a servo-throw adjustment that will allow you to match the servo throw with the carburetor-throw requirements.

9. If there isn't any electrical adjustment provided with your radio and the servo either over-controls or under-controls the throttle pushrod, move the ball link farther out on the servo arm for a greater throw or closer in to the center for less throw. Sometimes, the carburetor arm has more than one adjustment hole, so between moving the ball link at the servo and trying the different holes on the throttle arm, a position can be reached where full idle and idle trim will cut off the throttle and yet allow full-throttle operation without overdriving the servo.

GYRO INSTALLATION

The gyro senses yaw movement about the vertical axis, and it should therefore be mounted as indicated in the helicopter's instructions. If there isn't a specified place for the gyro, choose a place that protects it from mishaps, is fairly well removed from engine vibration and is clear of the engine exhaust's heat and residue. Mounting instructions differ, so check your specific gyro's instructions.

Before you mount the gyro on the helicopter, verify the proper operation and servo movement with the system hooked up as it will be for flight. Your gyro has a normal/reverse switch so the servo direction can be changed after it has been installed.

Checking gyro direction

Before you install the gyro in the helicopter, verify that it operates properly by following this procedure:

1. Connect the gyro, rudder servo, battery and receiver, following the gyro instructions.

2. Adjust the gyro's sensitivity control to approximately 50 percent of maximum. If the gyro has two sensitivity adjustments, set them both to the 50-percent setting because you'll use only one setting during initial practice sessions.

3. Turn on the transmitter, receiver and gyro, and move the rudder control on the transmitter right and left. Verify that the servo moves in the correct direction. The helicopter instructions should indicate which servo direction gives right nose movements and which gives left. Another way to check for proper servo movement is to watch the tail-rotor blades as you move the rudder. They must increase in pitch when a right command is given at the transmitter and vice versa. If necessary, use the servo-reverse switch in the transmitter to obtain the proper movement.

4. Now that the servo is moving the tail rotor correctly, look at the servo-output arm as you move the rudder stick on the transmitter to the right. Note whether the servo arm rotates clockwise or counterclockwise with a right stick command.

5. With the gyro on the table, rotate it sharply counterclockwise to simulate a left nose movement by the helicopter. The servo arm should move in the same direction as in the previous step to give a countering right nose command. If the servo moves in the wrong direction when you do this test, the gyro is giving a wrong input and its direction must be reversed. If the gyro has a reverse switch, move it to the other position and run the test again to verify that it operates properly.

Figure 10-7. The gyro sensor should be mounted using the supplied foam tape to minimize vibration.

Mounting a gyro

A common way to secure the gyro is with servo-mounting tape—a padded tape that has adhesive on both sides. The tape not only keeps the gyro in position, but it also protects it against vibration. The tape will stick well only to clean, dry, smooth surfaces, and it does have two disadvantages:

1. If you have to remove the gyro, you'll have to cut the tape because it's difficult to release the extremely strong adhesive. This leaves a sticky residue on both the helicopter and the gyro; you must scrape it off or rub it off with a cloth and lacquer thinner. This could not only mar the gyro, but it could also take some of the paint off the helicopter. To avoid having to do this, coat the bottom of the gyro and the part of the helicopter to which the gyro will be mounted with several strips of 3M Magic Tape—the kind that looks invisible when applied. I find this far superior to the regular (shiny) Scotch tape. The servo-mounting tape will stick to the 3M tape, which can then be peeled off cleanly when necessary, leaving a completely new-looking gyro and helicopter.

2. If the mounting surface isn't completely clean and dry or the tape itself is rather old, the adhesive might not be strong enough. This can cause the gyro to vibrate loose in flight, and you'll have some unwanted control inputs and possibly damage your helicopter. To prevent this from happening, I add two or three drops of CA (instant glue) to the tape when I mount it. By doing that, I ensure that it stays in place, and I can still peel it off with the tape.

Your gyro may have a separate on/off switch or sensitivity adjustment switches that are designed to be mounted on the helicopter. Mount these switches away from the engine exhaust and where they're easily accessible, even when the engine is running.

Figure 10-8. Some gyros have a separate control amplifier. This is used to change the gyro's direction and should be mounted so that it's isolated from vibration.

ON/OFF SWITCH

Following the manufacturer's instructions, secure the receiver's on/off switch to the helicopter. It should be mounted on the side opposite the engine's exhaust and where it's easily accessible when the engine is running. If I mount the switch vertical, I use the up position for "on" and the down position for "off" because this seems natural to me, and it's the way my light switches work at home. If the switch is horizontal and sticks out from the helicopter, I mount it so that the "on" switch position is to the rear. This ensures that if I ever hover/taxi close to the ground and something hits the switch, it won't turn it off. Admittedly, this is unlikely, but it's something to consider.

RECEIVER & BATTERY

Separately cover the receiver and battery pack in plastic wrap to protect them from water, fuel and dirt in a crash. Then separately wrap each with about ½-inch-thick foam rubber, and secure them in place with several rubber bands and zip-ties. Now position the receiver and the battery in the helicopter, following the instructions (use rubber bands, plastic ties, etc.). The receiver is especially delicate, and it's costly to repair or replace, so you must give it every chance to survive a mishap. Neatly secure the remaining wires with rubber bands or plastic ties, keeping them away from moving servo arms and the receiver antenna.

The receiver antenna must now be routed outside the helicopter to the bottom of the vertical fin. Keep it away from other radio components and the hot engine and exhaust. Do not wrap the antenna around itself to make it shorter because this will reduce its operating range.

Another option is to do away with the long antenna and use a whip antenna. This short wire antenna is base-loaded so the receiver thinks it's longer, and it can easily be mounted inside the canopy.

WEIGHT & BALANCE

Although we don't have a lot of control over the helicopter's total weight, we can adjust its overall center of gravity (CG) if we need to. With the helicopter built and all the equipment installed—but with an empty fuel tank—check the helicopter's CG by removing the main rotor blades and lifting the helicopter from the flybar. The CG can also be checked with the blades installed, but make sure that they're facing directly fore and aft. Your instructions should be specific about CG location, but in any case, the nose should tip

slightly forwards so that the rear of each skid is about ¼ inch higher than its front. You shouldn't have a rearward CG, or the nose will be higher than the tail. If you do, move the battery farther forward if you can to bring the CG within desired limits, or add a small weight to the nose. But remember, any weight added will detract from the helicopter's overall performance.

Having installed all the radio equipment, do another range check. With an assistant holding the helicopter about waist-high, turn on the transmitter and the receiver, and do the range check as you did before. When the maximum range is reached, have your assistant slowly move the helicopter around in a circle to see whether there are any "dead spots" in the reception. If the range has decreased or is less than

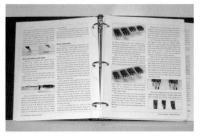

Figure 10-9. SR Batteries offers several volumes on electric RC flight techniques. They'll help you to understand your radio equipment and how to take care of it.

the minimum specified by the radio manufacturer's instructions, reposition the receiver antenna to obtain maximum range. You may also have to reposition the receiver, battery and wires to obtain the proper range. Again, if you can't get the proper range, do not attempt to fly the helicopter.

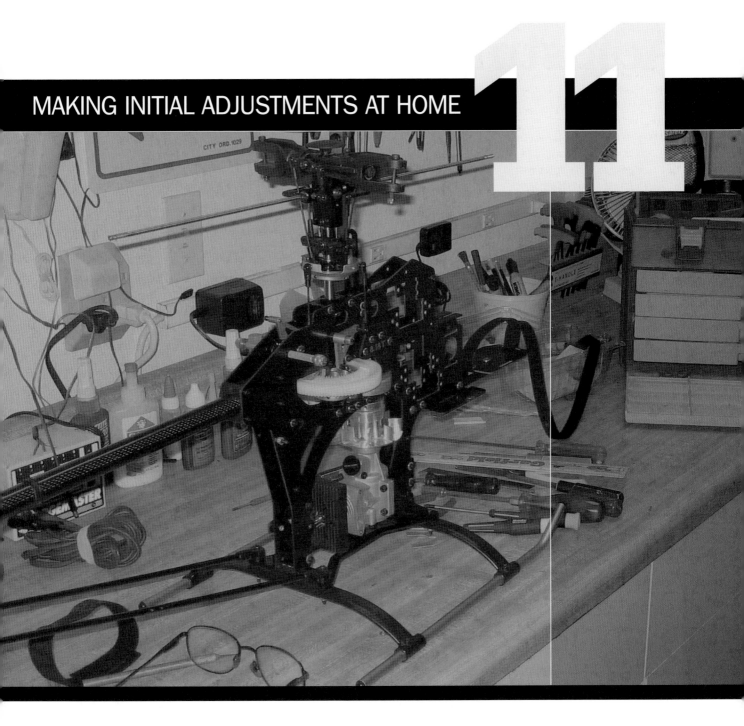

Making Initial Adjustments at Home

By now, you should be looking at your completed helicopter with a great deal of satisfaction, knowing that you installed all those screws, washers, bolts, bearings and parts and assembled something that looks like a helicopter and will really fly. And now you want to start the engine and hear it run and watch those blades go around. But try to resist that urge for the moment, and continue to take one step at a time, making sure that you do everything correctly the first time. Remember, you've invested a great deal of time and money in this helicopter, and your goal is to keep it in one piece and operating correctly so that you can learn to fly it.

Part of your building instructions will also cover initial setup, so reread that section carefully now. Most setup instructions assume, however, that you're an average flier rather than a novice, and they'll give you directions that result in a helicopter that flies well, rather than one that's tailored to your initial training needs. For this reason, I recommend a different setup from that described by the heli's manufacturer, but it will be better for hovering.

Throughout this setup process, take a few seconds to sit back and look at the big picture occasionally. Look at what you've accomplished, and ask yourself

Figure 11-1. Adjust the linkages according to the instructions. You'll fine-tune them when you test-hover.

whether it looks reasonable. Even though you don't have much helicopter experience, you do have a lot of common sense, and as I've said before, if something doesn't

look right, it probably isn't.

Much of the initial setup was done when you installed the radio, but now it's time to take a closer look at the controls and to fine-tune the adjustments—mechanically (the way the control pushrods are adjusted) and electronically (the adjustments on your radio). Put the helicopter on a workbench where you can turn it freely 360 degrees and where the rotor blades are also free to rotate as needed. If you haven't yet mounted the rotor blades, do that now and extend them to their usual flying position. Also, ensure that all the servo arms are at 90 degrees to the servos with the sticks and trims in their mid-positions (except for the throttle). All the other adjustments, such as servo throw, dual rates, etc., should be at their full or turned-off positions.

THROTTLE

Throttle setup is discussed in some detail in the section on radio installation, but we should revisit it now because it's important—not only for the proper operation of the helicopter, but also for your safety when you first start the engine. Turn on the transmitter and receiver, and run through these checks:

First check all control functions for freedom of movement. To do this, disconnect the throttle linkage/ball from the throttle servo. Hold the pushrod close to the servo in its normal position, and then push-pull as the servo would and check for freedom of movement. This is especially important at full open and closed throttle.

Next, match the servo throw to that required by the carburetor. With the pushrod still disconnected from the servo, bring the throttle and trim to the full idle or closed position. Move the carburetor to the fully closed position, and hold the pushrod against the servo arm in its normal position. Usually, a little adjustment is needed either to prevent the servo from over-

Figure 11-2. Check all the linkages for freedom of movement, and make sure that there isn't any slop in the control system.

driving the throttle arm or to bring the throttle to the fully closed position. But before you make any adjustments, check the servo/pushrod position in a similar manner at full open throttle. You can adjust the overall throw by moving the pushrod in or out on the servo arm and by adjusting the length of the pushrod. You should be able to get very close by making these adjustments. If further adjustments are needed, refer to your radio instructions on how to adjust the servo throw, or endpoints. Again, however, make these final adjustments with the pushrod disconnected from the servo to check for full movement without over-driving the servo. When everything is set properly, the servo should move the carbu-

retor through its entire range from fully open to fully closed without binding.

With the throttle stick and trim at their full idle (low) positions, the servo arm should be close to 90 degrees to the servo body, as described in Chapter 10. This will give the throttle trim maximum effectiveness and will allow the throttle to open quickly as the throttle stick is advanced. With the throttle stick and trim still at their lowest positions, is the engine carburetor in the fully closed, or cutoff, position? If it isn't, adjust it until it is. This is an important step because you must be able to shut the engine down in an emergency.

Advance only the throttle trim to its maximum position, and the servo arm should rotate slightly and cause the carburetor to open very slightly. On many engine installations, this is hard to verify, but if the carburetor arm moves approximately ⅛ inch, it should be sufficient. This small throttle opening is all that's needed for the engine to idle; you can adjust it further after the engine has been started. By moving it throughout its trim range, you can now use the throttle trim lever to adjust the engine's idle speed, and you will be able to cut the engine off at its full, low position. Some radios also have a throttle-cut button; it does the same thing as bringing the throttle trim to full idle. If you have

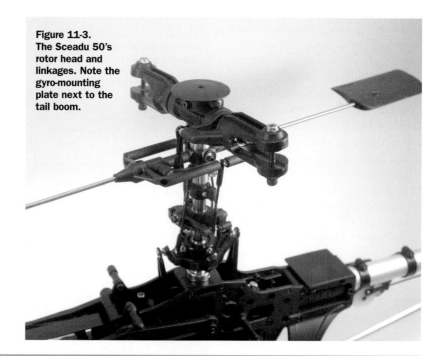

Figure 11-3. The Sceadu 50's rotor head and linkages. Note the gyro-mounting plate next to the tail boom.

Cyclic setup: aileron & elevator

When you installed the radio, the pushrods for the aileron and elevator were connected to the inner holes on the servo-output arm. For most helicopters, this will provide the required sensitivity—or lack of sensitivity—for initial training, but it can be checked further by using the following technique:

1. Disconnect the pushrod from the aileron servo, and move it back and forth in the same way as the servo would. It should operate freely throughout its full range of movement as the swashplate moves fully right and left.

2. Notice how much pushrod travel is required to make the swashplate move from full right to full left. If you set up your controls to give that much swashplate movement, the helicopter would be much too sensitive for training, so, to start, ½ or ⅓ of that movement should be satisfactory.

3. Connect the pushrod to the aileron servo, and turn the transmitter and the receiver on.

4. Move the aileron stick full right, and make sure that the swashplate tilts to the right (viewed from the rear of the helicopter). If it tilts to the left instead, refer to your radio manual and reverse that servo.

5. Move the aileron control stick from full right to full left, and see how much the swashplate moves. Is it about ½ (or slightly less) than the movement in step 2?

6. If the swashplate moves more than ½ of its movement in step 2, you can reduce it by using the aileron dual-rate function on the transmitter. Again, refer to your radio manual to turn the dual-rate function on. Flip the dual-rate switch to the "on" position, and adjust the aileron dual-rate to reduce the servo throw as required. Using dual rates will allow you to make small control-sensitivity adjustments when you start to hover.

7. If the swashplate doesn't move enough, move the pushrod farther out on the servo wheel. Move it to the next hole out from the center, and test again.

8. If the main rotor blades rotate clockwise, the swashplate should also tilt very slightly to the right (viewed from the tail) when the aileron control stick and trim are at neutral. And if the main rotor blade rotates counterclockwise (to the left), the swashplate should also tilt slightly to the left in a similar way. This slight control input is required to counteract the tail-rotor thrust. (See Chapter 12 for a detailed explanation of the effect of tail-rotor thrust on the helicopter.) The initial aileron-control adjustments are now complete.

9. In the same way, adjust the elevator control. But with the elevator stick and trim in their neutral positions, the swashplate should tilt very slightly towards the heli's nose. (This trim technique is discussed further in the chapter on hovering.)

such a radio, check to ensure that it does close the throttle completely.

TAIL ROTOR: RUDDER

You connected the tail-rotor pushrod to the second hole in the servo-output arm when you installed the radio, and that should be a good starting place for hover training. If your radio has a rudder dual-rate capability, you'll be able to use it later to reduce the tail-rotor sensitivity if required.

Adjust the tail-rotor pushrod so that, with the servo at neutral, the rotor blades will have a slightly positive angle of attack, or pitch. If you can estimate about 10 degrees, that should be fine; you'll make further adjustments when you start to hover.

GYRO

Rotate the helicopter's nose and notice how much tail-rotor-pushrod movement there is. The gyro should command about ¼ inch of total pushrod movement (about ⅛ inch in each direction). Adjust the gyro sensitivity as required to obtain this ¼-inch movement. This completes the gyro adjustment.

COLLECTIVE

Most helicopter setup instructions recommend a collective-pitch range of about -5 degrees to +10 degrees, and I agree with these

Figure 11-5. Tighten the tail-rotor blades only enough to keep them in position; they should be free enough to find their correct position as they rotate.

numbers if you plan the usual helicopter flying, but they aren't what I recommend for learning how to hover. Using these numbers for your setup could have two undesirable results:

• Having a maximum pitch of 10 degrees will allow your helicopter to climb faster than you're now able to control. An incorrect command from you could send it climbing quickly to a height of several feet, and you'll have to try to get it down in one piece. While you're learning to hover, there's never any need to be more than 6 inches to 1 foot off the ground. If you can hover at 6 inches, you can hover at 6 feet, but with wide training gear, you're unlikely to do any damage from 6 inches.

• Having 5 degrees of negative pitch available enables you to

descend rapidly when the need arises, but this is certainly not necessary, or desirable, while you're learning. Having negative pitch will allow your helicopter to screw itself into the ground if you make a mistake, and I've seen a lot of damage done in this way.

To avoid these two situations, set the total pitch movement at from 0 as a minimum to +5 degrees as a maximum. This has several beneficial results: the 5 degrees should just be enough to get the helicopter, with training gear, off the ground, but not enough to let it get so high that it could be in danger. This is also a good way to judge your rotor rpm; if your helicopter doesn't get airborne, the rotor speed is probably too slow, and this has other adverse effects, which I will discuss later.

The minimum of 0 degrees of pitch will allow the helicopter to descend but not quickly enough to damage itself, as long as it wasn't too high.

An additional benefit of this collective range is that the collective stick will be less sensitive and, therefore, more easily controlled. To hover the helicopter, the collective will have to be near its maximum position, and the helicopter will then barely get off the ground. When a descent is

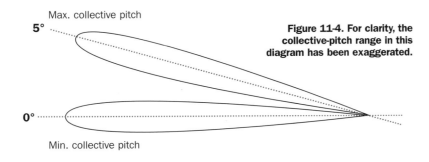

Max. collective pitch

5°

Figure 11-4. For clarity, the collective-pitch range in this diagram has been exaggerated.

0°

Min. collective pitch

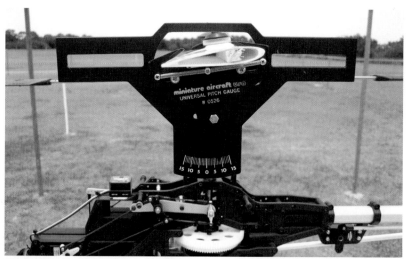

Figure 11-6. Using part of an old rotor blade to check pitch adjustments at the field.

required, it will take only a small decrease in collective to allow the helicopter to descend gently.

By using a pitch gauge, you'll be able to accurately adjust the collective pitch of both blades. But before I discuss the use of a pitch gauge, I'll discuss the gauge itself. It's important that the pitch-gauge readings be repeatable from one use to the next and that the gauge be easy to use both at home and at the field. Remember that the number on the gauge doesn't make the helicopter fly, but it's a starting point for other adjustments, and the use of the gauge will also allow accurate changes to be made. Also, when the helicopter is flying the way you like it, you can measure the pitch again at the high, mid-range and low collective points, and use these settings later after maintenance, etc.

With this in mind, use the following procedure with the pitch gauge to first adjust the collective-pitch range and then to set the high and low collective-pitch settings:

1. Again, turn the transmitter and receiver on, and put the heli on your workbench so you have a side view. The main shaft should look vertical, and the tail boom should be level with your workbench.

2. Use the elevator trim to level the swashplate. Note that the tilt of the swashplate in the aileron (right/left) direction has no effect on the collective-pitch reading when you look at the side of the helicopter.

3. Following the manufacturer's instructions, connect the pitch gauge to one rotor blade, and keep the flybar, swashplate and tail boom level for the next steps.

4. Bring the collective stick to its lowest position, and note the collective-pitch setting. To do this, hold the top or bottom of the pitch gauge level (it should be parallel to the flybar), and read the blade pitch on the gauge.

In a similar way, take the collective stick to its highest position, and again read the blade pitch. The difference between the high and low readings represents the collective-pitch range, or pitch window, which, for the initial setup, should be about 5 degrees. Note that right now, we aren't concerned with the actual pitch settings but with the pitch-range window. The high- and low-pitch settings will be adjusted shortly.

The collective-pitch window you just calculated is probably not 5 degrees, but it can be increased

or decreased mechanically (instead of electronically, in the transmitter) by changing the point on the servo arm where the pushrod is connected. Moving the pushrod closer to the center of the servo arm will decrease the window, and moving the pushrod farther away from the center will increase the window. Choose the servo-arm position that provides a 5-degree window (or slightly more).

When you've set the correct pitch window, adjust the maximum pitch to 5 degrees by changing the length of the pushrod going from the swashplate to the head (this will automatically make the minimum pitch about 0 degrees).

Adjust the second blade to correspond with the first both at high and low collective. These specific pitch settings (and the collective range) are just initial adjustments and will be refined later as you fly your helicopter.

Since you are not familiar with storing, handling, or transporting your helicopter, I recommend that you protect the main rotor blades by taking them off the helicopter and storing them in a protective bag. To protect my helicopter, I hang it from the ceiling using a hook and a home-made cradle made of clothes-hanger wire. Bend the wire into an inverted "V," and at a point that's wide enough to reach the flybar, form a hook on both ends of the wire. This cradle is strong enough to handle the weight of the helicopter, and it's very easy to remove it from the hook in the ceiling and from the flybar.

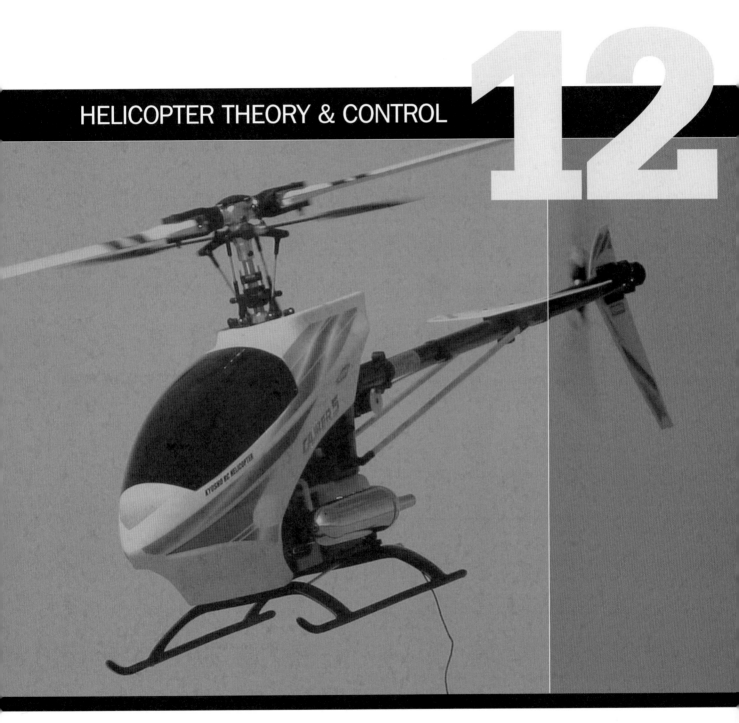

Helicopter Theory & Control

Until now, you've been building your helicopter and setting it up statically, i.e., on the workbench, without the engine running or the blades turning. The next step is to take it to the field, start the engine and set it up dynamically so that you can start your training. But before we get to that, it's important to discuss the basic forces that act on a helicopter and how you can control these forces with your radio to get the helicopter to hover, fly and maneuver. Helicopter theory can obviously be quite complicated, but my examples and explanations are rather general to give you a basic understanding of why helicopters do what they do. If this whets your appetite, you'll find many more advanced sources of scientific, in-depth explanations of helicopter flight.

Initially, I discuss the balance of forces on a helicopter while it's in a hover, and then I go into how a helicopter changes direction and altitude. The term "balance of forces" refers to the forces that act on the helicopter—pulling it up, down, or sideways. If the helicopter is hovering, all these forces must cancel one another out if the helicopter is to remain stationary. If they don't, the resulting force will make the helicopter move, and that's precisely what enables us to move and control the helicopter. I'll use a Mode 2 transmitter as an

example: the aileron/elevator is on the right stick, so while you read this, have your helicopter and radio nearby so that you can compare the theory with your helicopter. Now, turn on your radio, move the controls, and watch the reaction of the blades, paddles and linkages. As you progress, this will help you to understand what's happening to the controls and how that relates to your control-stick input on the transmitter.

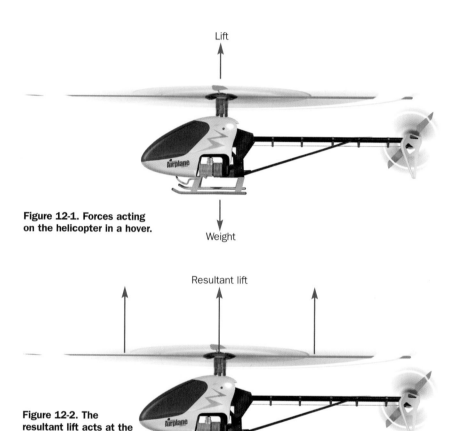

Figure 12-1. Forces acting on the helicopter in a hover.

Figure 12-2. The resultant lift acts at the center of the rotor disc.

BALANCE OF FORCES IN A HOVER

Side view. Figure 12-1 shows a side view of the forces acting on a helicopter in a hover. The arrow going straight down represents the force of gravity (weight) on the helicopter. This is counteracted by the rotor blades' lift; in a hover, lift equals weight, and the helicopter doesn't climb or descend. You don't have many options with regard to the force of gravity because it's just the sum of the weight of the helicopter, fuel, radio and equipment. But with the left stick, you can control the lift produced by the rotor blades. As the left stick is moved up towards the top of the transmitter, engine speed and power are increased, as is the rotor blades' collective pitch. Therefore, you control lift in a hover solely with the fore/aft movement of the left stick to keep the helicopter in a stationary vertical position. With your transmitter, practice moving the left stick up and down, and watch how it controls both the engine and the collective pitch of the rotor blades. But make sure that you aren't in throttle-hold or idle-up, or it won't respond properly.

There are two other important factors to note in Figure 12-1:

• The arrow that represents lift going straight up is shown acting directly over the main shaft. Actually, the main shaft has no lift capabilities; the lift is produced farther out on the blades, but the resultant force acts as if it were centered on the main shaft, as shown in Figure 12-2. This isn't important now, but keep it in mind as we discuss rotor blades further.

• The lift produced by the rotor blades is always perpendicular to the rotor disc (Figure 12-2).

Top view. Figure 12-3 shows the helicopter in a hover as we look at it from above. Again, all the forces that act on the helicopter from this perspective must cancel one another out to keep the helicopter stationary.

Newton's Third Law of Motion states, "For every action there is an equal and opposite reaction." Therefore, as the main rotor turns clockwise, the fuselage tries to turn counterclockwise. This ten-

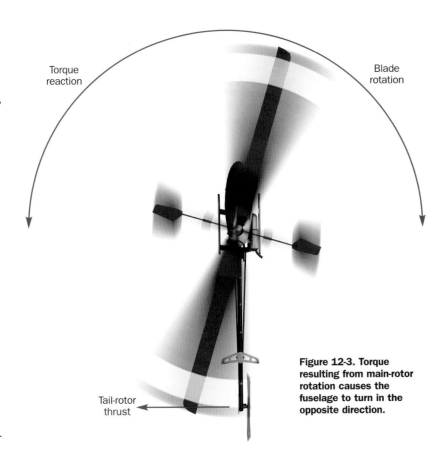

Figure 12-3. Torque resulting from main-rotor rotation causes the fuselage to turn in the opposite direction.

dency of the fuselage to turn is called torque, and any change in engine power or collective pitch brings about a corresponding change in this torque.

The tail rotor's function is to compensate for this torque reaction, and when the thrust of the tail rotor equals the force of the torque, the nose keeps pointing straight ahead. If the thrust of the tail rotor is increased to the left, the helicopter will rotate around the main shaft and cause the nose to go to the right. In a similar manner, a decrease in tail-rotor thrust will cause torque to take effect, and the tail will go to the right, or the nose to the left. Again, in a hover, all these forces balance to keep the helicopter pointing steadily in one direction.

The tail rotor's rpm depend on the engine/main-rotor rpm, which in a hover should be constant. The tail-rotor thrust is

therefore changed by increasing or decreasing the angle of attack of the tail-rotor blades, and on your radio, you do this by moving the left stick right or left. Look at the tail rotor from the left side of the helicopter; it will usually rotate to the right (clockwise) from this viewpoint. Now move the left control stick on your transmitter to the right, and see how the blades' angle of attack increases. This will cause the blades to take a bigger bite of the air and will cause the tail to move to the left, or toward you. As you move the stick to the left, the angle of attack will decrease, and the opposite effect of moving the tail to the right, or away from you, will occur.

Another important point has just been made, and this needs to be emphasized: although the left transmitter stick changes the tail-rotor blades' angle of attack to

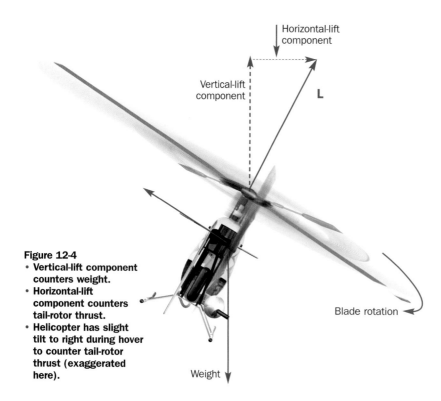

Horizontal-lift
component

Vertical-lift
component

L

Figure 12-4
- **Vertical-lift component counters weight.**
- **Horizontal-lift component counters tail-rotor thrust.**
- **Helicopter has slight tilt to right during hover to counter tail-rotor thrust (exaggerated here).**

Blade rotation

Weight

make the tail move right or left, the direction in which the tail moves is opposite that of the stick. The reason for this is that you don't "fly" the tail: you want to control the nose. Again, move the left stick to the right and the left, and convince yourself that when the stick is moved to the right, the nose will move to the right and vice versa.

Attempting to fly the tail is a very common mistake among new helicopter pilots, and it should definitely be avoided.

Rear view. Figure 12-4 shows the helicopter in a hover as viewed from the rear, with a greatly exaggerated tilt to the right for instructional purposes. Again, all the forces must balance to keep it in a steady hover.

From this viewpoint, we can again see the force of gravity pulling the helicopter down. As already discussed, this is again compensated for by the rotor blades' lift. But now, you'll also

notice something that you haven't seen before: the rotor is slightly tilted to the right. The lift is still perpendicular to the rotor disc but with a greatly exaggerated tilt to the right for instructional purposes. This lift can also be seen as having two components: a part that acts vertically and a part that acts horizontally. (This is the basis of vector analysis, which you might like to read about in a math book but which I won't discuss here). To keep the helicopter at a fixed altitude, only the vertical component of the total lift must be equal to the weight.

Now, let's leave the main-rotor disc to look at the tail-rotor thrust. Tail-rotor thrust will make the helicopter move to the left unless another force cancels it, and this is exactly the purpose of tilting the main rotor slightly to the right. Because the rotor disc is tilted to the right, part of the total lift is horizontal and to the right, and this force counteracts the

force from the tail rotor to prevent the helicopter from drifting right or left.

To sum up: the vertical component of lift counters the force of gravity, and the right horizontal component of lift counters the left thrust of the tail rotor. Because everything is balanced, the helicopter will remain in a stationary hover.

HELICOPTER MOVEMENT

Climbing & descending. Refer again to Figure 12-1, in which the rotor-blade lift equals the weight of the helicopter, so it therefore maintains altitude in a hover. To make the helicopter climb, we increase the lift until it's greater than the weight. Also, the rate of ascent is determined by how much of this "excess lift" is available.

Lift can be increased in two basic ways: by increasing the rotor speed or by increasing the pitch of the rotor blades.

A helicopter with a fixed-pitch rotor system must depend solely on rotor speed to climb and descend, but one with a collective-pitch system can keep the rotor speed fairly constant and can climb or descend just by changing the pitch of the rotor blades.

If you have a collective-pitch helicopter, turn on the radio and increase the collective; note that the rotor blades simultaneously increase and decrease in pitch. The way we have the helicopter set up, you'll see that there isn't much of a pitch change from maximum to minimum collective, but right now, you don't need much pitch change.

Another important factor pertaining to ascents is shown in Figure 12-5. This represents a helicopter (seen from the rear) that's about to lift off from the side of a hill. The slope shown is exaggerated to illustrate my point, but the effects are just as real on a gentle slope. Earlier in this chapter, I showed that the lift from the main rotor blades is always perpendicular to the rotor disc, and again, that's shown in the figure. But since the rotor disc is tilted along with the helicopter, any increase in lift will have a vertical and a horizontal component, as shown. In this case, this horizontal component will cause the helicopter to move to the left as it's brought into a hover. So if you try to lift into a hover from uneven ground, the helicopter will move in the direction of the slope, so it's therefore better to practice from level ground. If you have to take off from uneven ground, the rotor disc must be tilted to the horizontal plane to enable the helicopter to make a smooth, vertical liftoff. In this case, right aileron must be applied before liftoff and then, as the helicopter becomes airborne, quickly brought back to neutral to make a liftoff without side movement.

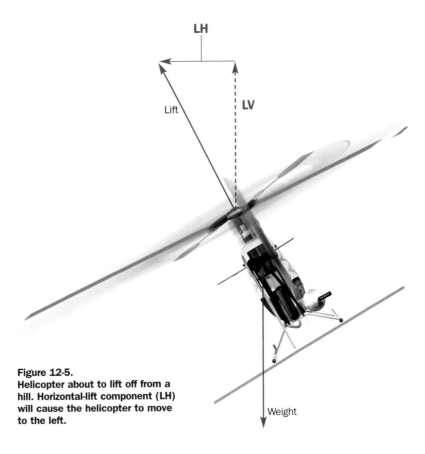

Figure 12-5.
Helicopter about to lift off from a hill. Horizontal-lift component (LH) will cause the helicopter to move to the left.

Transition to forward flight

Figure 12-6 shows a helicopter in transition from a hover to forward flight, and several important points are illustrated here:

• The total lift of the rotor blades comprises the lift produced by the front half of the rotor disc and that produced by the rear half. This is an important point that we haven't seen before, i.e., that lift can change in value from one section of the rotor disc to another. This basic idea is what enables the helicopter to change direction.

• The sum of the lift from the front and rear halves of the rotor disc equals the total lift, as shown in Figure 12-1.

Because the lift of the rear of

Figure 12-6.
Transition to forward flight—greater lift on rear portion of rotor disc.

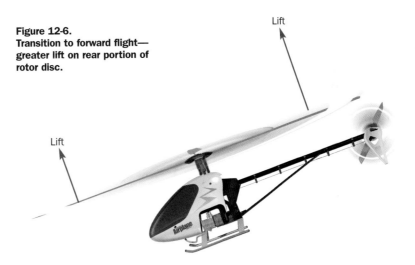

the rotor disc is greater than that of the front, the tail will rise and the nose will drop. This is commonly called "pitching forward." When the helicopter has pitched forward slightly (as exaggerated in Figure 12-7), the vertical portion of the lift must continue to equal the weight of the helicopter to keep it at a constant altitude; the horizontal portion of total lift determines how much force is available to propel the helicopter forward.

With the radio turned on, push the right stick forward to give full-forward cyclic (or down-elevator), and note how the swashplate

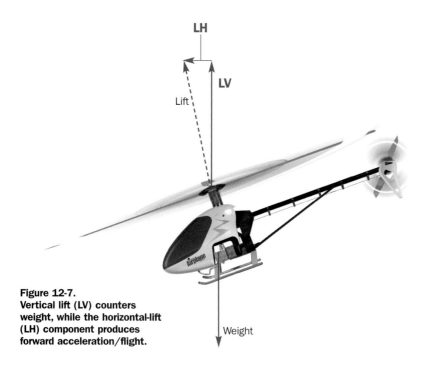

Figure 12-7.
Vertical lift (LV) counters weight, while the horizontal-lift (LH) component produces forward acceleration/flight.

Watch the tip of one rotor blade as it rotates slowly around the helicopter, and note how its pitch changes at various points around the circle. This change in pitch is called "cyclic pitch" (the change in pitch in one complete, 360-degree cycle of the swashplate), and it causes the lift around the rotor disc to change, depending on the commands given to the swashplate. As the pitch is increased, so is the lift, and this causes that portion of the rotor disc to have more lift than the other sections. Because of this, you'd expect to find maximum pitch near the rear of the helicopter to raise the tail, but if you look closely at the pitch change as the rotor blade turns, you'll see that maximum pitch occurs at 90 degrees before the rear of the helicopter, which is the left side for a clockwise-rotating system. This is the result of gyroscopic precession.

rotates forward. Bringing the stick back to neutral will level the swashplate, and pulling the stick back will give up-elevator and will tilt the swashplate to the rear. This movement of the swashplate controls the nose movement—up or down. (Pushing the stick forward will lower the nose, and pulling the stick backward will raise the nose.) To get a better

idea of how this is accomplished, push the stick forward to give full down-elevator. While the swashplate is tilted full forward, turn off the receiver and then the transmitter. The swashplate should now be tilted forward but be level right to left. Now we can analyze how the movement of the rotor blades gives this change in lift to produce forward flight.

GYROSCOPIC PRECESSION

The spinning main rotor acts like a gyroscope, and gyroscopic precession is the action of a spinning object when a force is applied. This action occurs approximately 90 degrees in the direction of rotation from the point at which the force is applied (Figure 12-8).

This means that the blade with the increased pitch will try to rise, but because of gyroscopic precession, it won't rise until approximately 90 degrees later in the plane of rotation. This is why the maximum angle of pitch is reached as the rotor blades pass the side of the helicopter, but the resultant force will be applied as the rotor blades pass the rear of the helicopter to tilt it forward.

Figure 12-8.
Gyroscopic precession: rotor blade produces a force at point A, but it reacts 90 degrees later in the direction of blade rotation (point B).

BANKING, OR SIDE MOVEMENT

In a similar manner, a change in lift from one side of the rotor disc

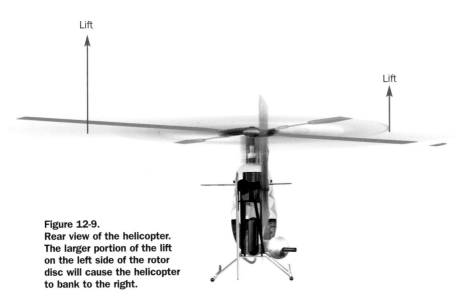

Lift

Lift

**Figure 12-9.
Rear view of the helicopter.
The larger portion of the lift
on the left side of the rotor
disc will cause the helicopter
to bank to the right.**

to the other will enable the helicopter to bank either to the right or to the left, as shown in Figure 12-9. Again, turn on your radio and move the right stick to the right and to the left, and note how the swashplate follows the control-stick movement. Moving the stick to the right makes the swashplate tilt to the right, and this will cause the helicopter to move in that direction. Moving the stick to the left causes the opposite reaction.

YAW

Yaw is the movement of the helicopter about its vertical axis, or main rotor shaft. Using one hand, pick up the helicopter by its head, on top of the main rotor shaft. With the other hand, move the tail from side to side. The right and left movement of the nose is called a "yaw movement," and it's controlled by the tail rotor. We've already seen how the tail rotor counteracts the helicopter's torque, but by changing the thrust of the tail-rotor system, we can also change the nose position, and this will allow you to point the helicopter wherever you choose.

Moving the left stick on your transmitter to the right and to the left controls the pitch angle of the tail-rotor blades. Look at your helicopter and move the left stick to the right to give right rudder. You'll see that the blades' pitch angle has increased, and this will increase lift in the horizontal plane. This increase in lift will cause the tail to rotate to the left, thereby causing the nose to rotate to the right. Note that moving the control stick affects the tail rotor, but the direction in which the

stick is moved corresponds to the direction in which the nose moves—not the tail. This is because you'll always look at, and control, the nose and not the tail.

GROUND EFFECT

When a helicopter is hovering at a height that's approximately less than the diameter of one rotor disc, it encounters "ground effect." This is where the downwash velocity created by the rotor blades can't be fully developed because of the proximity of the ground, so the helicopter rests on a "bubble" of higher-pressure air. A more detailed analysis of ground effect would deal with the rotor blades' induced angle of attack, the change in induced drag, and the corresponding change in the total lift vector. This is only mentioned to whet your appetite. You may be interested in this phase of helicopter flight, but a more detailed analysis is beyond the scope of this book.

In my limited experience of flying/hovering full-scale helicopters, a helicopter does handle differently when it encounters ground effect. It's almost like sitting on top of a balloon and trying not to fall off. Some model helicopter

Figure 12-10. A helicopter card optimizes control functions. Memory cards allow several models to be flown using one transmitter and allow you to experiment with—and save—multiple heli setups.

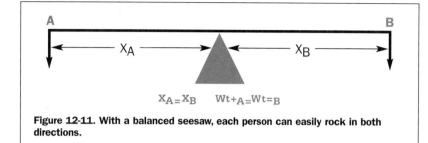

Figure 12-11. With a balanced seesaw, each person can easily rock in both directions.

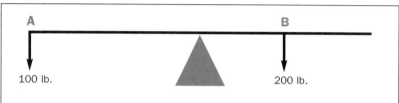

Figure 12-12. If one person weighs more than the other, the heavier person must move closer to the pivot point to balance the seesaw.

pilots say that they, too, can feel when their heli encounters ground effect and that it acts in the same way on their helicopters. But I can't tell whether I'm in or out of ground effect. The amount of ground effect is also determined by the wind; it will have maximum effect on a calm day and less effect as the wind's velocity increases to "push" the higher-pressure air from under the helicopter. This hovering in a wind brings us to the next topic.

TRANSLATIONAL LIFT
Translational lift is the additional lift obtained because of the rotor system's increased efficiency when in horizontal flight. This increased efficiency is the result of the higher in-flow velocity of the air, which supplies the rotor disc with a greater mass of air per unit of time than it gets while it hovers. This translational lift is present with any horizontal movement, and it increases as a function of the helicopter's velocity. The additional lift available is referred to as "effective translational lift," and it's easily recognized in actual flight by an improvement in the helicopter's performance.

Because translational lift

depends on airspeed rather than on ground speed, a helicopter doesn't have to be in horizontal flight to be affected by it. Translational lift will be present while it hovers in a wind, and the amount of additional lift is proportional to the wind's velocity. This additional lift can, however, be both a help and a hindrance. It's a help in that less power is required for hover and forward flight, but if the wind is gusty, flight will be erratic, as the lift increases with any increase in wind speed and decreases as the wind subsides. For this reason, it's important to practice hovering only when the wind is steady—preferably at 5 to 10mph.

AUTOROTATION
This is the term used for unpowered helicopter flight, i.e., when the engine has failed and the main rotor continues to turn because of momentum and because of the action of the wind on the rotor blades as it descends. When the engine powers the main rotor for normal flight, the flow of air is downward through the rotor disc. When the engine has stopped in flight, however, and a helicopter enters an autoro-

tation descent, the flow of air is upward through the rotor disc. This upward flow of air and the negative pitch in the rotor blades cause the rotor to continue to turn and allow the helicopter to be controlled as it descends. The rotor system in helicopters with autorotation capability has a one-way clutch that allows the main rotor blades to continue to turn even though the engine has stopped. It isn't absolutely necessary for a model helicopter to have an autorotation capability, but if it doesn't, the main rotor will stop rather quickly if the engine fails during flight, and a crash involving major damage will be unavoidable.

TRIMMING THE FLIGHT CONTROLS
Figure 12-10. When a helicopter is brought into a hover, to remain stationary, it must counteract the many forces we've already discussed, and this usually means holding right aileron to counteract the tail-rotor thrust, or holding down-elevator to counteract the effects of the wind. It would be very difficult (and tiring) to hold the control sticks continuously off-center to keep the helicopter in a hover, and for this reason, the radio has trim levers next to the control sticks.

Turn on your radio, slowly move the aileron stick to the right and watch the servo movement. Now bring the stick back to center and slowly move the aileron trim lever to the right (the trim lever is below the aileron stick), and again watch the servo movement. You'll notice that moving the trim to the right moves the servo about 10 degrees to the right, but the aileron stick remains in its neutral position. This means that if you're in a hover and the helicopter wants to drift left slightly, you can counter that by moving the aileron trim lever to the right slightly until the helicopter maintains its lateral position with the aileron stick in neutral. This gives you a reference from which to fly, it relieves you of continuously holding the stick in the off-center position, and it allows you to concentrate on the other controls. Exactly how far you move the trim lever will depend on your helicopter's initial setting and on the forces involved; if full trim movement still isn't enough, land the helicopter and adjust the linkage. The trims for the elevator and rudder operate in a similar way. Just remember to move the trim lever in the direction in which you must hold the control stick to make the helicopter hover.

BLADE BALANCING

Two rotor-blade balancing techniques are presented in Chapter 9, but to understand them better and to develop your own techniques, it's important to have a basic understanding of balance theory.

I'm sure we all played on a seesaw when we were children; I'll use this to demonstrate many balance requirements. Figure 12-11: the idea behind a seesaw is to place two people of equal weight the same distance away from the pivot point. This represents a balanced seesaw that each person can operate easily to rock in each direction. If one person weighs more than the other, however, there is a problem: the seesaw tips towards the side with the heavier person.

Let's suppose that one person weighs 100 pounds, while the other weighs 200 pounds. To balance the seesaw, the heavier person must move closer to the pivot point, as shown in Figure 12-12. And if you think that the heavier person should move halfway in, you're correct. But

why? Certainly, it seems right and looks right, but there's a mathematical explanation.

Refer to Figure 12-13, which shows the original balanced seesaw. The reason it's in balance is that its clockwise moment is equal to its counterclockwise moment, with "moment" being defined as a force acting over a certain distance. Notice that the person on the left weighs 100 pounds and is 10 feet away from the pivot point. The resulting moment is therefore:
100 lb. x 10 ft. = 1,000 ft.-lb. (in the counterclockwise direction). And because the person on the right side of the seesaw is the same weight and the same distance away from the pivot point, he also produces a moment of 1,000 ft.-lb., but now in the clockwise direction. Because these moments are equal and opposite, the seesaw is in balance.

Now look at Figure 12-14—the second example. The person on the right has been replaced with someone who weighs 200 pounds and sits halfway to the pivot point. The counterclockwise moment is still 1,000 ft.-lb., as in the previous example, and the clockwise moment is:

200 lb. x 5 ft. = 1,000 ft.-lb. (in the clockwise direction).

So, again, the seesaw is in balance because the moments are equal and opposite. This proves mathematically that what we thought to be right is indeed correct.

Well, now that we have learned something about a seesaw, what does it all have to do with balancing rotor blades? Referring to Figure 12-15, which shows two rotor blades in balance about a pivot point, notice that the weight of blade A (as shown at

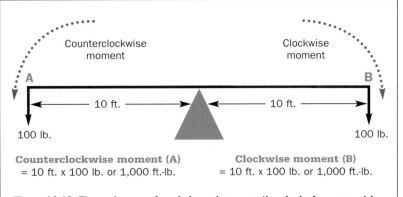

Counterclockwise moment (A)
= 10 ft. x 100 lb. or 1,000 ft.-lb.

Clockwise moment (B)
= 10 ft. x 100 lb. or 1,000 ft.-lb.

Figure 12-13. The real reason for a balanced seesaw: the clockwise moment is equal to the counter-clockwise moment.

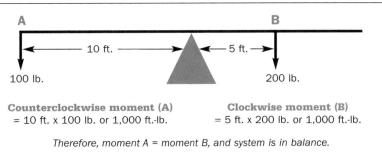

Counterclockwise moment (A)
= 10 ft. x 100 lb. or 1,000 ft.-lb.

Clockwise moment (B)
= 5 ft. x 200 lb. or 1,000 ft.-lb.

Therefore, moment A = moment B, and system is in balance.

Figure 12-14. Because the heavier person has moved halfway towards the pivot point, the moments are equal and opposite, and the seesaw is balanced.

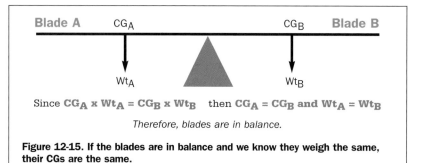

Since $CG_A \times Wt_A = CG_B \times Wt_B$ then $CG_A = CG_B$ and $Wt_A = Wt_B$

Therefore, blades are in balance.

Figure 12-15. If the blades are in balance and we know they weigh the same, their CGs are the same.

the blade's center of gravity [CG]) is the same as the weight of blade B. Also, the distance from the pivot point to each blade's CG is the same.

And just like the seesaw, we know that the blades are in balance because:

If weight of blade A = weight of blade B, and CG of blade A = CG of blade B; the moment (weight x CG) of blade A = the moment (weight x CG) of blade B.

The blades are therefore in balance and ready to be installed on your helicopter.

But let's suppose that your rotor blades are similar to the second seesaw case in which the blade on the right is heavier than the one on the left, but the CG has been moved closer to the pivot point to match the moments. Are the blades still in balance? As long as the moments are the same, the answer must be yes, but I think it's also quite obvious that these rotor blades would not work well on a helicopter because they will be out of balance when they are spinning.

This can be demonstrated by attaching a small, relatively light stone to a string and spinning it above your head. It will produce a certain force. Now take a heavier stone, attach it to a shorter string, and again spin it above your head. Are the two forces equal? Even if one stone weighs twice as much as the other and the string

is half the length, the dynamic forces will not be the same. Therefore, if we used such different blades on a helicopter, it would certainly be out of balance.

So, we can now say that not only must our blades balance statically (the blades are not moving and the moments are the same), but they must also balance dynamically (while spinning). Clearly, the only way we can obtain both a static and a dynamic balance is to have the weights and CGs of both blades be the same. If we can do this, we will know that our statically balanced blades will also be in dynamic balance on our helicopter.

In Figure 12-15, notice that if the blades are in balance (level) and we know that they weigh the same, we can therefore deduce that their CGs are the same. In a similar manner, if the blades are again in balance and their CGs are the same, we can deduce that their weights are the same. This is very important because now, all we need to guarantee a set of perfectly balanced blades are any two of the following:
• Their weights are the same.
• Their CGs are the same.
• They balance level.

The preceding paragraph is very important, and it's the conclusion of the entire discussion on blade-balance theory, so please reread it to be sure that you understand it completely. Any blade-balancing technique must guarantee at least two of the three requirements, so choose a tech-

nique that produces the most accurate results with the least work and cost.

The blade-balancing technique I have found to be the most accurate and cost-effective is to use a combination of the first two balancing requirements—matching two blades in weight and CG. Small, inexpensive digital scales (available at office supply stores) can weigh a rotor blade to within $\frac{1}{10}$ gram. But I have used only one product to determine a rotor blade's CG accurately, and that is the Koll Rotor-Pro balancer.

First, weigh each blade to determine which is heavier. Then place the lighter blade on the scales and add electrical tape, blade-covering material, etc., until the blade's weight equals that of the other blade. Now we know that the equal-weight requirement has been met.

Using the Koll Rotor-Pro balancer, find the CG of the heavy blade. Then put the light blade on the balancer and move the tape as needed to match its CG to the heavy blade's. When you've determined the correct position for the tape, be sure to wrap part of the tape around the blade's leading edge so that the airflow does not lift the tape during flight. Now we know that the second requirement has also been met, and therefore, the rotor blades are in balance and ready for flight.

Although many rotor blades are sold as balanced and ready to fly, this balancing technique is so easy and quick that there is no reason not to check every set of rotor blades before you use them. A few minutes with the scales and a balancer can save you a lot of vibration at the flying field.

CARBURETOR ADJUSTMENTS

Definitions. Although there are many different brands, sizes and types of model engines, each with its own unique carburetor, their adjustment procedures are very similar. Your particular engine/carburetor combination may look a little different from what I present here, but by reading the manufacturer's instructions and using these techniques, you'll be able to adjust your engine with very little effort.

HELICOPTER TERMS

Rich: having adequate or plentiful fuel. You can "richen" the fuel mixture by turning the needle valve counterclockwise.

Lean: having less fuel. You can "lean" the fuel mixture by turning the needle-valve clockwise.

The knee of the curve: that is what I call the diagram in Figure 12-16. The "rich" engine in section A is running in a 4-cycle condition and producing very little power. You can tell the engine is in a 4-cycle by the large quantity of exhaust smoke, the low-frequency exhaust sound and the lack of rpm and power. This area of the power curve isn't suitable for helicopter operations because of the low engine rpm and power.

As the needle valve is closed (turned clockwise), the engine is leaned out to section B on the curve. You will hear the engine enter a 2-cycle by an increase in exhaust-sound frequency, an increase in power and speed and a decrease in exhaust smoke. As the engine just enters a steady 2-cycle, I refer to this as a "rich" 2-cycle, and it's an ideal mixture for most types of helicopter operations. The engine produces good rpm and power and is also receiving a suitable amount of lubrication and cooling fuel.

As the needle valve is closed further, the engine continues to lean out and enters section C of the curve, which I refer to as a "lean" 2-cycle. Notice that the power curve increases in this area and is suitable for those who require maximum rpm and power from the engine such as for 3D and contest flying. The danger when operating in this area of the curve, however, is that the engine is dangerously close to section D.

As the needle valve is leaned further, the engine enters section D. Now the engine isn't getting enough fuel, and this results in a loss of rpm and power, overheating and a reduction in useful

engine life. This is obviously not the place to be, but because there is no well-defined line between section C and section D, many fliers find themselves operating in this section without knowing it. This is why I recommend that you try to stay in section B so you have a margin for error in your adjustments.

ADJUSTMENT TECHNIQUES

Every carburetor has a main needle valve, and it does exactly what its name implies. It is the main controller of how much fuel enters the carburetor, and since all other adjustments are a function of its setting, it must be adjusted first. Also, when you first start your engine, you would like to be in section A or B of the curve and not in C or D. The engine's instructions should give you initial settings for the main needle valve and the idle needle valves. If there aren't any instructions, leave the idle needle valve set at the factory setting, and open the main needle valve about 3 turns.

To start the engine, fuel the helicopter and position it so that the fuel line that goes to the carburetor is facing you. Then, with the electric starter, turn the engine over for a few seconds. You should see fuel in the line going to the carburetor. When fuel enters the carburetor, stop turning the engine over, or you will flood it. Now connect the glow-plug battery to the glow plug.

Put your transmitter within easy reach and make sure that the throttle stick is at idle with the idle trim advanced slightly. Securely hold one blade grip with one hand while you start the engine with the electric starter using your other hand. Always be cautious: the engine could start at a high power setting for some reason, so have a firm hold on the rotor head. If this does happen,

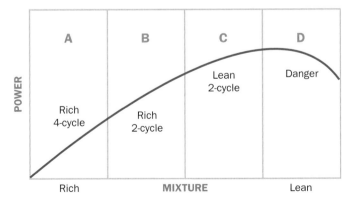

Figure 12-16. This "knee of the curve" diagram illustrates rich and lean engine operation. Try to stay in section B so that you have a margin of error for your adjustments.

make sure that the throttle stick is at idle, and if it is, pull the fuel line out of the engine to stop it.

Having started the engine, don't be too concerned with the idle-mixture setting as long as the engine runs. Remember, your first job is to adjust the main needle valve. To do this, stand well clear of the helicopter and advance the throttle until the helicopter is light on its skids. I hope the engine is in the 4-cycle range (section A of the curve) or at least in a rich condition. Bring the throttle to idle, wait for the rotor blades to stop turning, and then approach the helicopter and immediately seize the rotor head with one hand. Close the main needle valve about ⅛ turn and again bring the helicopter to where it's light on its skids. Continue this engine-leaning procedure until you are in a steady 2-cycle condition (section B on the curve).

With the main needle valve adjusted, bring the engine to idle and again secure the rotor head. Now you can get an idea of the idle-mixture setting by pinching the fuel tubing that goes to the carburetor (use your fingers or needle-nose pliers) and listening to the engine. If the idle mixture is set correctly, the engine rpm should increase for 2 or 3 seconds, and the engine should then start to die because it lacks fuel. Release the fuel line to keep the engine running at idle.

If the engine accelerates for more than a 3 seconds, the idle mixture is too rich. Close the idle needle valve ⅛ turn and do the pinch test again.

If the engine accelerates only for a second or so when you pinch the fuel line, or if it starts to die immediately, the idle mixture is too lean. Open the idle needle valve ⅛ turn and do the pinch test again.

When you think you have the idle mixture set correctly, stand away from the helicopter and see how the engine accelerates from idle. If it does so smoothly and returns to a good idle, the idle mixture is correct. If the engine hesitates and produces a lot of exhaust smoke, it's running too rich. If the engine fails to return to a normal idle from a higher speed, it usually means that the idle mixture is too lean.

As you experiment with these adjustments and get to know the sound and feel of your engine, you'll be able to set it very accurately, and you'll feel confident that it's in the desirable "knee of the curve" section.

Safety

When someone talks about safety, do you think, "Oh no. Not that again," or "I'm safe; this is a waste of time," or something similar? Every helicopter kit comes with a warning that the helicopter is not a toy but something that must be respected for its potential dangers if it isn't operated properly. If we take steps to make our hobby safe, it enhances our enjoyment of it and also benefits everyone at the flying field. Paying due attention to safety prevents us from injuring our friends and ourselves and helps us avoid damaging our equipment.

Many think that safety starts when the transmitter switch is turned on, but it starts well before that—all the way back to when we start to build the helicopter. If we can build the helicopter better, not only will it perform better and provide more enjoyment, but it will also be inherently safer to fly.

Building safety

These are some points to consider when you build; maybe you can add to the list.

• Read the instructions. In the instruction manual, manufacturers go to great lengths to detail the best possible way to assemble their products. If you follow the instructions to the letter, your helicopter will perform as it was designed to, and it will be a safer machine overall.

• Take your time when you build. When we get a new kit, we all want to get into the air, but rushing is a sure way to make a mistake that will eventually cause a crash, or worse.

• Use Loctite on everything that doesn't have a lock washer, and don't overtighten. The Loctite will prevent setscrews and bolts from vibrating loose, and over-tightening can actually distort parts, strip threads, round off hex wrenches and make maintenance and repairs even more difficult if you can't disassemble the part when you need to.

• After completing a building sequence, recheck the tightness of the screws, bolts, etc. In some steps, the parts are not fully tightened immediately but are only "finger tight" until later in the construction, when other parts are brought into alignment. Failing to properly tighten these parts is obviously just as bad as over-tightening them.

• Balance parts that rotate, and lubricate all the moving parts when you build. This will result in a smooth flying, long-lasting helicopter.

• Route radio wires away from sharp edges and engine and muffler heat.

• Don't redesign the helicopter as you build it. Although a minor change may look good to you, you assume that a manufacturer failed to see your potential for improvement. In most cases, manufacturers have tested your ideas themselves and rejected them to produce the best overall design.

• Install the on/off switch where it can't accidentally be turned off. If it's vertical, make "up" the "on" position, because that's what we're used to when we turn the lights on at home. If it's horizontal and it's easily reached from outside the helicopter, make "back" the "on" position, in case you hover over tall grass or weeds that could move the switch back.

When the construction is complete, it's time to take care of the machine in which you've invested so much money, time and effort.

Maintenance "musts"

• To prevent moisture from getting into the bearings, keep the helicopter away from damp areas such as a basement or garage. I put a blind bolt in the ceiling of my workroom, make a hook out of a clothes hanger and hang the helicopter out of the way near the ceiling.

• One of the best ways to find little problems before they become big problems is to clean your helicopter. Wrap a cloth around a finger, and clean off all the fuel residue. Look for a residue of dirty oil and tiny metal or plastic flakes created by vibration; this indicates a loose bolt, a broken joint, etc.

• Always fully charge the transmitter and receiver battery packs before you fly. Even if you flew only a flight or two on the last day you flew, put the packs on charge overnight to make sure that they're ready to go. Use a digital voltmeter, and note what the packs' voltages are when they're fully charged. Any decrease in this full-charge voltage could be the first sign of battery problems.

• Periodically cycle the transmitter and receiver packs with a commercial cycler. Cycling the packs eliminates any memory buildup and tells you the pack's capacity. Any decrease in capacity is also a sign of problems.

• Make preflight inspections. Although you should check and clean your helicopter at the end of every flying session, give the helicopter a once-over and check the battery-pack voltage before you fly.

• Most rotor blades can be folded into the blade grips for ease of carrying and transportation. Take care when you fold the blades; support them to relieve any weight they might put on the head linkages or servos.

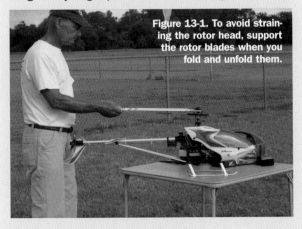
Figure 13-1. To avoid straining the rotor head, support the rotor blades when you fold and unfold them.

• Don't lift the helicopter by grasping the head. Doing so would put your fingers on the flybar and various pushrods, and that could alter some head adjustments. Instead, lift the helicopter using one or both blade grips. They are designed to handle the weight of the helicopter, and you'll keep your hand clear of all linkages, ball links, etc.

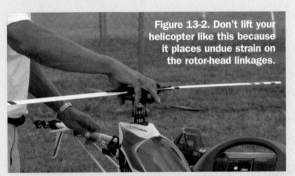
Figure 13-2. Don't lift your helicopter like this because it places undue strain on the rotor-head linkages.

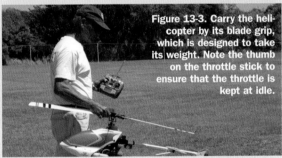
Figure 13-3. Carry the helicopter by its blade grip, which is designed to take its weight. Note the thumb on the throttle stick to ensure that the throttle is kept at idle.

• When your heli is in your car, secure it and the radio, fuel, starter and all the other heavy items so that they can't move or turn over when you turn a corner, etc. Put the heavier objects toward the front and against the back of a seat, in case you have to make an emergency stop. Put the transmitter in a container that will protect its many switches.

Figure 13-4. The padded Heli-Max rotor-blade bag has room for two sets of main blades and tail-rotor blades. High-quality blades such as the V Blades and Thunder Tiger blades shown here will last much longer when protected during transportation.

Flying-field safety

Some fliers design a test stand or attach their helicopter to a table to adjust blade tracking and to dynamically set up the engine and rotor blades. I don't recommend a test stand because you make adjustments close to the helicopter while the rotors are turning. If the test stand isn't absolutely stable or something comes loose, you could be severely injured.

I hope you'll never need it, but it's always smart to have a first-aid kit available. Unfortunately, many of our flying sites are well away from other people, so also have a cell phone and know the directions to the nearest hospital emergency room.

When you're ready to start the engine for the first time, I recommend that you first remove the main rotor blades. If the throttle is accidentally set above idle, the engine could start at a power setting that's higher than anticipated, and it will try to spin the rotor blades while you're standing very close to them. Also, engine-mixture and carburetor-linkage adjustments are easier to make without the rotor blades' getting in the way.

As you become familiar with your engine and helicopter, develop a checklist you can use every time you go to the flying field. This good habit will ensure that you don't overlook small things that could prove harmful to you or your helicopter.

Keep your helicopter and other equipment off the ground where they could get dirty or be damaged. A simple folding table works well for this.

Range-check the radio equipment as specified in the radio manual. Do this with the helicopter off the ground and away from metal objects and with all of its parts in their normal flying positions (e.g., canopy in place). If you can't get the minimum range recommended by the manufacturer, or any part of the radio does not operate properly, do not attempt to fly or even hover. Not only will your radio not fix itself in flight, but whatever the problem is, it will also get worse.

Figure 13-5. The first time you start your heli remove the rotor blades. Run the engine at low speed only.

Before you start the engine

• Recheck the transmitter switches to ensure that the idle-up and throttle-hold functions are off.

• Hold the head firmly in case the engine starts at a setting above idle.

• Have the fuel line facing you so that you'll be able to remove it from the engine quickly, using a hooked finger, if you need to during a starting emergency.

• Use the starter extension carefully to avoid damaging the head linkages.

When the engine has started, take the helicopter well away from the starting area before you run up the engine.

Whenever the engine is running, guard the throttle stick at idle with your left thumb. I have had wind gusts blow my shirt and neck strap onto the throttle stick; this caused the engine to advance to almost full power while I was holding the head.

Figure 13-6. In an emergency, you can quickly shut down the engine by pulling off the fuel line.

Figure 13-7. When you handle the transmitter, keep your thumb over the throttle stick to prevent your neck strap, shirt, etc., from hitting the stick and advancing the throttle. The Petal RC transmitter tray provides great support while you're flying.

Figure 13-8. When you start an engine, keep a firm grip on the rotor head in case the engine starts at above idle. Note the proximity of the transmitter and the fuel line side of the heli—away from the exhaust, and toward me in case I need to shut down the engine quickly.

Fly safely!

• Never fly alone. In case you have an accident, there should always be someone who can assist you and go for help if needed.

• Stand well away and to the side of the helicopter as you advance the throttle. I've seen fliers standing only a few feet from their hovering helicopter. This is not safe! A malfunction or a gust of wind could cause it to move quickly and without warning. I therefore recommend a distance of about 15 feet between you and your helicopter at all times when the blades are turning.

• Wear a hat and sunglasses when needed. On bright sunny days, you might fly the helicopter towards the sun. Wearing sunglasses and blocking the sun with the brim of your hat could help you to avoid crashing.

• When you fly, take the wind, sun and terrain into consideration. Plan to do your maneuvers well away from spectators, trees, buildings, etc. A strong wind could push your helicopter into a dangerous position.

• Have a spotter, if needed, to watch for other helicopters and airplanes in your vicinity.

• Fly well away from other airplanes, helicopters and spectators.

• Everyone—not just the designated club safety officer—should be a flight-safety "official." Most clubs have a safety officer, but it's really a job for everyone. Rather than running for the safety officer—or just shaking your head if he isn't there—correct a dangerous situation yourself.

• Do a post-flight check and cleanup. Use a cloth wrapped around your finger to clean the helicopter after flight and, at the same time, inspect the helicopter for signs of minor malfunctions before they become more severe.

By looking closely at your helicopter, flying site, etc., you will be able to add to this list, I'm sure.

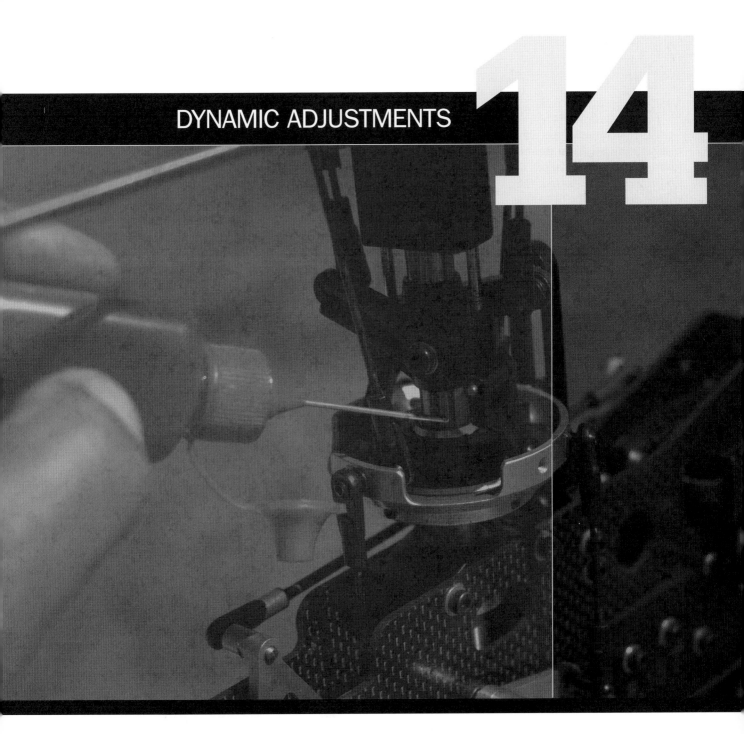

DYNAMIC ADJUSTMENTS

14

Dynamic Adjustments

Though you make initial adjustments statically on your workbench and without the engine running, before you can practice hovering, you have to start the engine and bring the helicopter into a hover, or at least get it light on its skids, to fine-tune your earlier adjustments. This is where it helps a lot to have the assistance of an experienced model helicopter pilot. I strongly suggest that you contact someone at the nearest RC airplane club or call local hobby shops to get the names of other heli fliers in your area; they can help you to get started.

If you have experience with model airplanes, you've probably heard of a plane that "flew right off the board," i.e., with no further trim adjustments. If this has ever happened with a helicopter, I've never seen it or even heard of it, so be prepared to spend time and effort on getting all the bugs worked out so that your helicopter will fly smoothly and properly. Success comes by following these instructions and taking the time to learn properly. Try to have someone help you to hold the helicopter when you start the engine and to work with you on the adjustments.

Where should you test your helicopter? A large, level, hard surface is best because the training gear will be able to slide on it, and this will make it easy to detect any movement without having the helicopter leave the ground. I recommend a large paved parking lot when there aren't any cars around,

Figure 14-1. If you keep your helicopter and its associated equipment on a portable table, you'll find it much easier to start the engine and make adjustments than when it's on the ground.

such as on a Sunday morning. Failing that, try to find a level field where the grass is short, and it won't catch the skids.

Pick a day that has a gentle, steady breeze of about 10mph (15kph). This breeze will keep the vertical fin and the nose pointing into the wind and, therefore, you won't have to concentrate as much on the rudder control. Don't pick a gusty day because sudden gusts could cause the helicopter to jump into the air and be tossed about.

Before you leave for the flying field, make sure that your batteries are all fully charged because making adjustments takes a long time.

AT THE FIELD

Set up the table, put the helicopter on it, and extend the rotor blades to their normal flying position. If you're at a club field, before you turn on your radio, check the club's frequency-control procedures. Also, see whether you can find an experienced club member to help you with the following adjustments:

• Turn on the radio, make sure that all the servos work properly, and range-check the radio according to its manufacturer's instructions. To do this, collapse or remove the transmitter antenna (depending on the instructions), and have your assistant watch the swashplate as you move the control sticks and walk away from the helicopter. Note the distance at which the servos begin to jitter and no longer respond to your control. This is the distance to use for the range check. Your radio's instructions will give you the minimum distance at which the radio should work with the transmitter antenna disconnected or collapsed. If it doesn't meet this minimum range requirement, the radio must be serviced by a qualified technician. Under no circumstances should you start the engine or attempt any further adjustments until the radio works properly.

ENGINE ADJUSTMENTS
Before you adjust the helicopter, it's important that the engine be operating properly. This means that you have to adjust the high- and low-speed needle valves for proper power and idle and for the transition between the two. For safety, it's also important to have the throttle set so that you can stop the engine by using the throttle stick and the throttle trim, as previously discussed. Before you start the engine, you must have a basic understanding of how the engine, its main valve, its idle needle valve and its carburetor work. This will help you to analyze any problems you might have with the engine's operation and help you avoid having to make unnecessary adjustments. This was discussed in some detail in Chapter 12, "Theory and Control."

• If no other instructions were provided with your engine, open the needle valve about 2½ turns out from fully closed to ensure an initially rich fuel setting. Fuel the helicopter with fresh fuel. I also use a filter in the line between the gas and the helicopter to keep out even the smallest particles. Even slight contamination can cause engine problems and may block the carburetor so badly that it won't get any fuel. When the helicopter has been fueled, be sure to close the fuel can tightly; it's important to keep out moisture, which will ruin the fuel. White specks in the fuel are a sign of water contamination or lubricant separation.

• From a safety point of view, if you aren't familiar with your engine or its settings, consider removing the main rotor blades. Even without the rotor blades, you can start the helicopter safely, place it on the ground and run the engine up to a moderate speed to make your initial carburetor adjustments. Without the rotor blades, it's easier and safer to approach your helicopter and stop the head from turning when you need to adjust the carburetor. When the engine is under control and needs only minor final adjustments, reattach the rotor blades to the head.

• Turn the radio on and make sure that the servos operate properly and that the transmitter switches are in the correct positions. Set the throttle stick to full low and set the throttle trim to its midrange position. This setting should allow the engine to idle without engaging the centrifugal clutch, but you may have to adjust it for higher or lower rpm after you've started the engine.

Figure 14-2. Have a helper check the rotor-blade tracking while you control the helicopter.

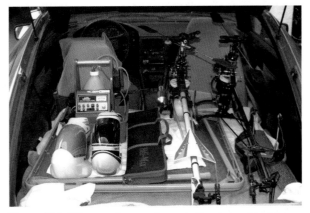

Figure 14-3. When you transport your helicopter, put heavier items at the front of the car. Here, the canopies have been removed to protect them.

• Put the transmitter within easy reach so that you can make trim adjustments after you've started the engine. Connect your glow igniter to the glow plug. If your battery system has a power panel with a meter that shows current, its needle deflection will indicate whether you have a proper connection and a good glow plug. If the meter needle doesn't move into the proper operating range, the power panel may have an output adjustment. If the needle doesn't move at all, there's a problem with the battery, the power panel, or the leads from the power panel to the engine, or the glow plug is defective. Most often, the glow plug is the problem, so check the system using a new plug.

• Before you engage the electric starter, be sure to grip the head securely with one hand just in case the engine starts at a throttle setting that's higher than anticipated. This sometimes happens with new engines because the throttle linkage is poorly adjusted. For your safety, it is vitally important that you hold the rotor head no matter what happens with the engine. The rotor blades could accelerate very quickly and be lethal to you and those nearby.
• Also, as another safety precaution, start your helicopter in such a position that the fuel line that goes to the engine is facing you. Then, if the engine starts at anything above idle (and it will, periodically), your first reaction will be to look at the transmitter to make sure that the throttle stick is in the idle position and that the idle-up switch is not engaged. If everything with the transmitter looks correct and the engine is still running too fast, hook your finger around the fuel line and pull it off the engine. This will stop the engine in a second or two.

• If your helicopter has to be started from the top through a starter cone, keep the electric starter and its extension as vertical as possible. This will allow a smooth power transfer between the electric starter and the helicopter, and it will prevent the starter extension from wobbling. It's very common for the electric starter extension to wobble during starting and even to hit the linkages that go to the head. If this happens, be sure to inspect all the linkages prior to flight to ensure that nothing was damaged.

• If your electric starter turns the engine over but fails to start it, the engine might not have enough fuel, or the glow plug might not be "glowing." First, prime the carburetor with a few drops of fuel, and then try to start the engine again. If the carburetor is hard to reach, you can prime the engine by using muffler pressure. To do this, first remove power going to the glow plug because we don't want the engine to start at this time. Then move the throttle stick to its full open position; this will bring the carburetor to the richer main needle-valve setting. Then put one fingertip over the muffler's exhaust while you turn the engine over with the electric starter. This action will pressurize the fuel tank, and that, in turn, will force fuel into the engine. Do this only for 3 to 5 seconds, or the

Figure 14-4. The large screens on some computer radios are easy to see, and they provide a good view of the adjustment functions.

engine might get too much fuel—an over-rich condition. If the engine still fails to start (or fails to show any signs of firing), check the glow plug visually if you don't use a meter to monitor the electrical circuit. Remove the glow plug and attach the battery leads to see whether the plug glows red-hot. If it doesn't, the plug, the battery, or the connections are defective. With sufficient fuel and a good "glow," the engine should at least start, but you may have to adjust throttle trim to keep the engine running.

• When the engine runs smoothly, adjust the throttle trim for a high idle without engaging the centrifugal clutch. Then disconnect the battery and carry the helicopter well clear of the starting area and away from other people to run further tests. Position the helicopter on level ground facing into the wind.

• The first adjustment will be to the engine—more specifically, to its main needle valve. It's important to remember that the main needle valve is the engine's primary controlling adjustment and must, therefore, be set first. Begin by increasing the throttle to get the helicopter light on its skids, but never let it leave the ground during these initial tests. When you advance the throttle, you'll probably notice vibration. The nose will try to swing in one direction or the other, and the rotor blades may be slightly out of track. You'll adjust all of this later; first, it's important to get the engine operating properly and reliably.

If you have a ringed engine, adjust it to a 4-stroke setting, i.e., so that the exhaust puts out a lot of smoke, and the engine sounds rather rough and generally lacks power. Right now, you aren't interested in getting maximum

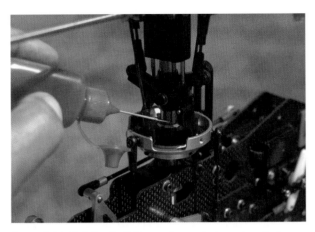

Figure 14-5. Lightly oil all the moving parts to ensure their freedom of movement.

Figure 14-6. Take a pitch gauge to the field to make pitch adjustments (rotor blade partially shown for clarity).

power from the engine; your concern is to run it rich to break it in, give it more than adequate lubrication from the fuel and protect it from overheating. If, however, the engine is of the ABC variety, don't run it in this 4-stroke condition; a 2-stroke setting will ensure that all the parts operate at their design temperature so they'll wear in properly. This 2-stroke setting is characterized by less smoke from the muffler, a noticeable increase in power and rpm and a smoother engine sound. But never rely on the amount of exhaust smoke to set the mixture. The volume of smoke depends on several factors, including the amount and type of oil mixed with the fuel, the type of muffler used and the temperature of the exhaust/muffler. You might see smoke coming from the exhaust and still have the mixture set too lean.

Because your engine is probably rather rich with our initial setting, bring the throttle back to idle, stop the rotor blades, and turn the main needle valve clockwise by ⅛ turn to the lean position. Move back and stand well clear of the helicopter, and again run the engine and check its operation. Do this until the main needle valve is set properly.

To adjust the idle needle valve, while gripping the rotor head with one hand, bring the throttle to idle and, with your other hand, pinch the fuel line that goes to the engine. The engine should speed up for 2 to 4 seconds and then start to die. Remember to let go of the fuel line before the engine dies, or you'll have to start it all over again. If the engine rpm don't increase, or they increase only slightly for a second or two and then start to die, the idle needle valve is set too lean. Open the idle needle valve ⅛ turn (don't adjust the main needle valve any further), and try the pinch test again. Continue to make slight adjustments until it's set correctly. If the engine accelerates for longer than 4 seconds during the pinch test, the idle setting may be too rich. If the engine hesitates or even quits when the throttle is advanced above idle, this also indicates that the idle setting is too rich. The excess fuel gets onto the glow plug and cools it, thus stopping the engine. Close the idle needle valve ⅛ turn and try the pinch test again, making further small adjustments as necessary.

BLADE TRACKING

Next, adjust the main rotor blade tracking. Increase the rotor speed until the helicopter is light on its skids, and have your helper bend down to look at the rotor tips.

When the blades are spinning, the colors of the tape on each blade should be superimposed on each another. Check this with the helicopter light on its skids to get all the flex out of the head and rotor blades and obtain a true reading. If the color of one blade looks higher than the other, bring the engine back to idle, stop the rotor blades, and either adjust the high blade downwards or raise the low blade. Generally, if you want to increase rotor rpm at hover, you lower the high blade, and the reverse is true if rotor rpm are too high. With the engine set to the rich side, however, you shouldn't have excessively high rotor rpm. The helicopter instructions should indicate which linkage you need to adjust to obtain proper blade tracking, and one complete turn on the clevis will usually make about an ⅛-inch change in rotor-blade position. Continue to increase rotor speed until the helicopter is light on the skids, and check for proper tracking; make minor adjustments until one blade (or color) is superimposed on the other.

TRIM ADJUSTMENTS

While you're doing these tracking tests and making adjustments, you could adjustment cyclic and tail-rotor trim. As the helicopter gets

Figure 14-7. Never touch the flybar or linkages while you're holding or moving a helicopter. Note the wheel collar on the far side of the flybar for balance.

Figure 14-8. Carry the helicopter tail-first, and you won't bang it into anything.

light on its skids, it should lift straight up. If its rotor disc is tilted to one side or if one side of the training gear is getting lighter before the other, adjust the cyclic trim to keep the helicopter level while you make these adjustments.

The change in rotor rpm (and, therefore, torque) between idle and hover rpm will also cause the nose to move to the right or to the left. This is quite usual because the tail rotor is trimmed only for a hover. As the helicopter gets light on the skids, hold the nose into the wind with the tail rotor, and adjust the rudder trim as needed.

VIBRATION

The adjustments already detailed should reduce any vibration your helicopter may have had. If there's still vibration, the main rotor blades, the flybar, the tail rotor, or the starter shaft may be out of balance or alignment. You'll generally notice vibration in the skids or the tail fin, but the front of the canopy is also a good indicator.

If there's very little vibration but it's also very fast and you see it in the tail fin, it could be coming from the tail rotor because it's rotating at very high rpm. Check the tail-rotor blades. If they've been adjusted too tightly, they will not extend to their normal

positions. If they're adjusted too loosely, they will vibrate.

Lower-frequency vibration is usually associated with the main rotor—more specifically, with the main rotor blades because they have the greatest mass. This vibration is usually seen as landing-gear shake or the tail boom vibrating up and down. To eliminate this source of vibration, add a little weight to the light blade, at its CG, to balance the system. Now the problem is to determine which is the light blade! At the field, there's really no practical way to determine which blade is lighter, so just pick a blade, assume it's the light one, and run a strip of electrical tape once around it at its CG. If your guess was right, the vibration should diminish or vanish. If you picked the wrong blade, the vibration will be worse; take the tape off the first blade, and run a new piece around the other blade at the CG. As long as you reduce vibration by adding tape, keep adding tape at the CG until the vibration disappears completely or you reach a point at which it increases. Any further vibration is probably the result of the flybar's being out of balance. To dynamically balance the flybar, move one of the flybar weights, or wheel collars, about ¼ inch from its

present position and see whether that helps. If it doesn't, move that weight back to its previous position, and move the other weight. A little trial and error with adjustments will give amazing results. There really isn't a scientific way to get it right the first time. Using the correct building techniques will, however, keep initial vibration very low, and one of the techniques I describe will help you to almost completely eliminate it. Admittedly, it can be rather tedious and frustrating, but work slowly and consistently, making only one change at a time so that you can evaluate its results.

The final step is to make linkage adjustments to center all the trims on the transmitter. You've probably had to move all of them off-center while you made your adjustments; if you don't center them, they could be moved accidentally, and you won't be able to remember all their exact positions. Again, this will be a trial-and-error process to figure out how many turns of the linkage it will take to return that particular trim to neutral. When you've done all this, it's time to start your hovering practice.

Hovering

It has taken a while to get here, but this is what all the building and planning were for—to see light under those skids. But this is also the time when you have to be particularly careful and patient. Resist the urge to "get started"—to fly before you're really ready. It's natural to want to fly, but it's easy to go too far too quickly and damage the machine you have cherished for so long.

With this in mind, your number-one goal is not really to learn how to hover but to keep the helicopter in good mechanical condition so that you will have something to practice with. I have seen many people try to learn too quickly and crash. They could have avoided this if they had tried to learn at a more reasonable pace. Remember: if your helicopter is down for repairs, you can't learn to fly it, so your number-one goal is to avoid damaging your helicopter. Learning how to hover is your second goal.

With all the building and setup behind you, this is a time when you expect to progress very quickly, and unless you have trained on a flight simulator, it can be mildly discouraging to find that helicopters are not as simple as they may seem. But there isn't anything like flying a helicopter. No matter what your life experience—even if you've flown a full-size helicopter—trying to master an RC helicopter takes skills and coordination that you have never had to draw on before. Don't expect success to come

Figure 15-1. This is the standard hover position: 30 degrees off the tail, about 15 feet away and facing parallel with the helicopter. Note that the transmitter antenna points in the same direction as the helicopter. The transmitter tray enhances a relaxed flying style. Practice looking at both sides of the helicopter.

overnight; in fact, I would be surprised if you had any real control over the helicopter going through your first few tanks of fuel. Sometimes, your helicopter seems to have a mind of its own, especially if it's out of balance and trim. But with patience and proper training, you'll soon learn to hover and fly.

One of the best habits to get into is to perform a thorough preflight check—at least, before the first flight of the day. In the last chapter, you have already learned how to make dynamic adjustments, and a full preflight may not be needed right now, but certainly, look the helicopter over and check for anything that may have vibrated loose. Every brand

and model of helicopter has certain areas that have to be watched, and the idea is to find these areas on your machine before you do any damage.

In Chapter 1, I discussed my techniques for holding the transmitter sticks. If you have not read Chapter 1 recently, I suggest that you reread it now, as you are ready to begin your hovering practice.

First, fill the fuel tank and check the transmitter to make sure that all of the switches and trims are in their proper positions. Then start the engine and carry the helicopter to the training area; put it on the ground facing into the wind. Stand behind the helicopter and about 30 degrees to the side, as shown in Figure 15.1. This is what I call the "standard hovering position," and it's where you should return after each attempt at hovering. Initially, it doesn't matter whether you stand to the right or the left of the helicopter because I will ask you to move from one side to the other to make sure that you don't favor one particular side. What does matter right now is that you have a good enough view of the helicopter to see small changes in attitude and make any corrections required, and you're in a position to get out of its way if you lose control. Do not stand any closer to the helicopter, and don't have people near you when you practice. They'll distract you or get in your way if you need to move fast.

THE GROUND HOVER

You will practice on a hard surface such as concrete or a softer surface such as grass. Each requires a particular technique as you begin to hover, so I'll discuss them separately.

Hard takeoff surface. With the helicopter facing into the wind, move to the standard hovering position already described. As you add power and collective, one of the helicopter's first reactions will be to yaw (turn its nose to the right or left). This is because the main rotor blades produce torque, and the helicopter reacts to that before the tail rotor has got up to speed to counteract it. Remember that when you adjusted the tail rotor, it was for hover rpm. Yawing is normal, but be prepared for it so that you don't think anything is wrong and start to change the trim settings. Instead, use the left stick to keep the nose straight as you add power; you can even add and reduce power slightly to give you a chance to practice with

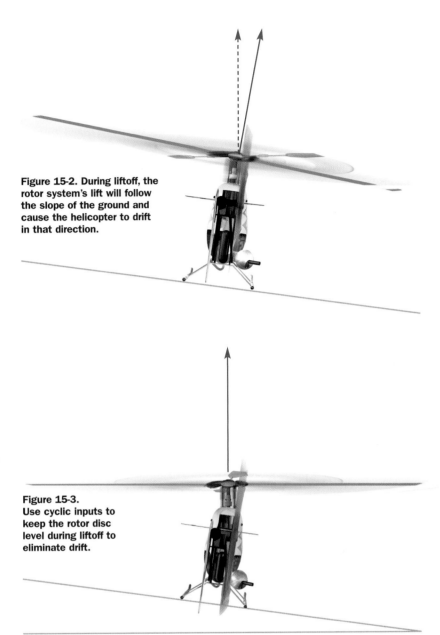

Figure 15-2. During liftoff, the rotor system's lift will follow the slope of the ground and cause the helicopter to drift in that direction.

Figure 15-3. Use cyclic inputs to keep the rotor disc level during liftoff to eliminate drift.

the left stick (rudder). Always remember to look at—and fly— the nose and not the tail.

If you practice in a light, steady breeze (and without the use of a heading-hold gyro), the large vertical fin will also help to keep the nose pointing into the wind, so there will be less need for control on your part.

As you continue to add power and collective, the helicopter will get light on its skids, and because the ground probably isn't completely level, there's a breeze, the

helicopter is slightly out of trim, etc., you will notice the helicopter starting to drift slightly. Counter this drift with the cyclic controls. But because the rotor speed is rather low and there is still weight on the skids, it will take a lot of correction to stop the drift or to get the heli to move in another direction. If you've set everything correctly, the helicopter will barely get airborne with full power and collective. If it lifts off, just decrease the collective trim slightly so that it will only slide around on the pavement and won't leave the ground. The only thing that will hurt your new helicopter is hitting the ground, so let's keep it on the ground and just slide it around while you get a feel for the controls.

At first, the helicopter will move on its own, and you won't really be able to counter its movements. Don't be discouraged; it's normal and is part of learning. But after a few seconds—not minutes—of trying to gain control, bring the throttle back to idle and think about what happened and which control response you made. Were you watching the nose? Is the nose still pointing into the wind? Are you moving the control stick in the direction in which you want the helicopter to move? Are you coordinating aileron and elevator for proper control? Remember that if the surface is not level, the helicopter will want to go downhill, and you will have to counter this (Figure 15-2).

For now, just try to get a feel for the controls. Later—perhaps several tanks of fuel later—try to keep the helicopter in one area and make it move in the direction you command. As you gain confidence and when you have some control over the helicopter, it will be time to get it slightly airborne, but more on that in a minute.

Grass takeoff. Much of the information given in the section on a hard surface applies to flying off grass as well. The helicopter will not, however, be as free to drift because of the drag of the grass. This means that you will have to get the helicopter a little lighter on the skids before there will be any movement. But initially, I still recommend that you adjust the collective trim to keep the helicopter on the ground at full throttle. I recommend this

Figure 15-4. The dark tape on this Sceadu 30's white rotor blades helps to define the rotor disc.

Figure 15-5. Hovering the Sceadu 30 with training gear at the Manatee RC field in Florida. Note the small fenced areas to protect pilots while others are flying; the large fence protects the flightline.

because you can do some very good early training by watching the training gear and the main rotor disc. As you add power and collective, look to see whether the rotor disc is horizontal. How about the training-gear legs? Are they all bearing the same weight, or are one or two bending because the helicopter is tilting to their side? Move the aileron and elevator control sticks slightly and see how it affects the rotor disc and the load put on every leg of the training gear. Your goal now is to get a feel for the controls, learn to increase power and collective and keep the helicopter's weight the same on all the training-gear legs.

Also notice that because the grass holds the helicopter in position, you barely have to control the tail rotor. Again, move the nose around as the rotor speed increases, and if it is light enough, it will move. And when you can make corrections automatically without thinking, it's time to think about getting the helicopter just slightly airborne. But don't be in a hurry to progress to hovering.

You'll find it a lot easier to hover when you have a good basic understanding of the helicopter and its controls, and you've practiced looking at the helicopter and transferring what you see into the proper control movements at the transmitter. It may take several practice sessions for you to feel comfortable with this, so progress at your own pace. A lot will depend on how much time you can devote to training and how often you can practice during the week.

FIRST HOVER ATTEMPTS
Now that you have a feel for the controls and the helicopter's response to control inputs, you are ready to get the helicopter off the ground. When some people think of hovering, they have visions of taking the helicopter smoothly up to 4 or 5 feet right away; this is a sure way of having to learn how to make repairs early. Your first attempts to hover will be at only several inches off the ground and for only a few seconds. Increase the hovering time

as you gain confidence, but still keep the helicopter low to avoid doing any damage. Remember, if you can hover at 1 inch you can hover at 1 foot, or at 10 feet, or at 100 feet. The helicopter handles the same at almost all altitudes.

Put the helicopter in front of you, go to your regular hover position, and slightly increase the collective-pitch trim. Then smoothly add power and collective and get to the now-familiar position of having the helicopter light on the skids. Then increase the collective ever so slightly, and the helicopter will lift off—straight up, if you're lucky, but that isn't very likely. As the helicopter leaves the ground, it may tilt for the reasons already mentioned, and it's your job to counter that and to keep the helicopter in the correct hover position. Try for a couple of seconds, and then bring the helicopter back to the ground and analyze your progress. Did the helicopter try to go one way or the other? If it did, how did you correct it? Did you make the proper correction or not? What will you do better the next time? Do the trims need adjusting? If they do, move the appropriate trim slightly in the direction that's opposite to where the helicopter wants to go, and try the control response again.

Now it's time to try it again, but again, just lift slightly off the ground for a short time. As you continue to progress, you will gradually be able to keep the helicopter off the ground for longer periods of time, but you will still feel that you have little, if any, real control over its movements. This is completely normal, so don't be discouraged. It will come, and then you'll be surprised by how easy it is.

Do's & don'ts

Between tanks of fuel, rest for a few minutes and go over some of these basic points.

DO'S

Relax. If you concentrate too hard, you may have a death grip on the transmitter, and then it will be almost impossible to get a feel for the sticks and make the proper response. And don't twist or lean in the direction in which you want the helicopter to move. Stay loose. Even if you think you are relaxed, have a friend watch you while you practice to assess whether you really are relaxed. It's hard to relax at first, and your friend may let you know where you're tensing up.

Stand erect with your arms hanging comfortably and the transmitter held easily, but firmly, in your hands. Keep your head and body straight; your leaning could be transferred into unwanted control movements.

DON'TS

Don't quickly add or cut power. This could cause the helicopter to get too high and then come down too hard and get damaged.

Don't ever try to back up or let the tail drop lower than its normal hover position. This is the major cause of tail-boom strikes because the helicopter will almost surely descend as the tail is allowed to drop, and the helicopter will hit the ground tail first. The tail rotor will be damaged, and the main blades will strike the tail boom. This is why I had you tilt the swashplate slightly forward during initial setup—to build in a little nose-down trim. If the helicopter moves forward on its own, certainly add up-elevator to try to stop it, but quickly correct back to the level position when the movement is stopped.

Don't ever practice when you aren't in your usual position in relation to the helicopter. You should always be in the proper position to reinforce the feeling of control you have, even if at first you don't feel you have much control at all. If the helicopter turns right or left or lands farther away from you, turn it into the wind and walk to your proper hover position before you try anything else. Be sure to practice hovering from both sides of the helicopter, or you will get a liking for one side or the other, and this is a bad habit that you'll have to break later.

Don't ever look at—or fly—the tail. Remember that the tail-rotor control is to correct the nose position. But the spinning tail rotor is all too easy to watch; don't let yourself get into this bad habit. Always focus on the back of an imaginary pilot's head, and be aware of the position of the rotor disc. Wherever the rotor disc tilts, the helicopter is sure to follow.

ADVANCED HOVERING

At this stage of learning, "advanced" hovering means flying the helicopter out of its hover position and bringing it back again. Don't attempt this until you are fairly proficient at hovering in a somewhat fixed position. I don't mean that you have to be able to keep the helicopter in a dead-still hover, but you should be able to keep it within a 3-foot circle (about 1 meter). When you can comfortably do this, you can increase the helicopter's altitude to about 3 feet or so, and, again, get comfortable with the helicopter at this height while you maintain control within the area mentioned.

Also, before you move the helicopter away from its usual hover position, be sure that you understand its basic movements and know which control responses to make to alter or correct them. To illustrate: let's suppose the helicopter is in a stationary hover and a gust of wind causes the nose to drop slightly. This, in turn, causes the helicopter to move forward slightly, and your initial reaction is to raise its nose back to the level hover attitude. But this level hover attitude will not stop the helicopter's forward movement, and you have to make a further aft cyclic command to raise the nose slightly higher and stop the forward movement. And when the helicopter is again stationary, you must drop the nose slightly back to its normal hover position. This means that you made three distinct control responses to make one very minor correction to the pitch axis, and certainly, other corrections to the other flight axes will also be required, at the same time. As you can imagine, it can be very difficult to figure out which correction is needed and how much correction to make.

But let's go back to the helicopter in a stationary hover for another demonstration. Again, a gust of wind causes the nose to drop, but you realize this before the helicopter has a chance to move, and you immediately make an aft cyclic correction to raise the nose back to its hover position. In this example, the helicopter didn't move, and it required only one correction to regain its normal hover position. And this anticipation is exactly what you should strive for as you practice: make the proper correction before the helicopter has a chance to move. This takes a lot of practice, but it's important to understand the prin-

Figure 15-6. This is trouble waiting to happen. Although the RotoPod training gear will protect the helicopter, allowing the tail to hit the ground will result in a boom strike.

ciple behind hovering and to get a feel for the helicopter's overall attitude so that you'll eventually be able to make a correction the instant it's required.

Once you feel comfortable in a hover, fly the helicopter about 2 meters farther away and to the side, and hover at that position. When you feel that you have complete control in that unfamiliar position, bring the helicopter back to its normal hover position. Then do the same thing on the other side, still keeping the helicopter about 2 meters away from you.

As you gain experience, you'll be able to move the helicopter increasingly farther away in this side movement until you feel comfortable when it's about 5 meters or so away from you. Then, instead of hovering at that point, return it to the normal hover position; and then do the same on the other side. This practice will help you learn how to keep the helicopter under control as it moves and changes directions but is based on a familiar position.

When you can make the helicopter move to the right and left away from you and bring it back, it's time to start incorporating the tail rotor into your practice. As the helicopter starts to move to the right from its normal hover position, add a little right tail rotor to let the nose swing slightly—and I mean slightly—to the right. Then, as the helicopter reaches the position farthest away from you, bring it back, but add a little left tail rotor to again swing the nose around in the direction in which it is flying. As you progress in this way, you will soon be able to move the helicopter to the right and left as you coordinate with the tail rotor to fly a figure-8 in front of yourself.

When you can fly this figure-8 comfortably, you have mastered one of the hardest parts of helicopter flying. There's certainly a lot more to learn, but this is the foundation for everything else, and you'll now have more fun as you gain control of the helicopter and learn its many maneuvers.

Repairs

Figure 16-1. Convert an inexpensive fishing box into a toolbox, and take it to the flying field in case you need to make adjustments and do minor repairs.

You should think about repairs before you need to make them. No matter how careful you are with your construction and flying, a mechanical malfunction, radio failure, interference, or pilot error will probably cause a mishap that will necessitate a repair.

During your initial training, you'll hover very close to the ground and use training gear that will minimize any crash damage.

As you progress, however, you'll eventually take the helicopter several hundred feet into the air, and a crash from that height will cause considerable damage.

For this reason, be prepared for such an eventuality and have a plan. Keep certain spare parts on hand, and take steps to minimize the damage if you do crash.

Must-have spare parts

- Set of main rotor blades
- Flybar
- Main shaft
- Tail boom
- Vertical fin
- Horizontal fin
- Assortment of 2mm and 3mm nuts, bolts and washers

Recovering a damaged heli

You should also know how to recover your helicopter properly to minimize the initial damage and prevent it from being further damaged. Copy the following steps, and take them with you whenever you fly:

1. If the engine is still running, attempt to shut it down immediately by bringing your radio's throttle and throttle trim to the full idle position.

2. If the radio malfunctions or the receiver has been disconnected and you can't stop the engine in this way, you'll have to walk over to the helicopter; approach it carefully. Hold the head to prevent it from turning, then pull the fuel line that goes to the carburetor so that the engine will be starved of fuel and will stop in a few seconds.

3. Once the engine has stopped, you'll feel an almost uncontrollable urge to pick the helicopter up and take it back to the pit area. Don't do this! Leave it where it is. There are certain precautions to be taken to make sure that you don't damage the helicopter further and that you have all the ejected parts. I have seen people take their helicopters back to the pit area, only to find out later that their receivers, battery packs, etc., are missing and that they can no longer accurately pinpoint the crash site to look for the missing parts.

4. Turn the radio off immediately. I hope it isn't damaged, but this is not the time to check your radio.

5. If the receiver and battery pack have been dislodged, disconnect their leads, and keep the items protected in their foam wraps. Be especially careful not to pull on the receiver antenna; untangle it gently, wrap the antenna wire around the receiver, and secure it with a rubber band.

6. If a servo has been knocked off its mount, don't let it hang by the pushrod or electrical wire. Doing so could break the wire or cause further damage to the gears or other parts of the drivetrain.

7. Even minor crashes can cause the fuel tank to split or leak around the fittings. The radio equipment must be protected from the fuel, and that's why I recommend that you keep the receiver and the battery pack in their foam wraps. If fuel is leaking, disconnect the fuel lines and either let the fuel drain out or take the tank out of the helicopter. Don't try to save this fuel because it could be contaminated.

8. When the helicopter is secure, check the immediate area to make sure that you have the receiver, the battery, the gyro and all the servos. Don't move the helicopter until all the individual pieces have been accounted for. A radio part may have been thrown some distance from the crash site, so widen the area to be checked.

9. Check that all the pushrods from the flybar and swashplate are still connected to the head. If any were thrown off in the crash, you may find them very close to the crash site. Look carefully within a 6-foot radius of the helicopter for any missing parts.

Figure 16-2. Although you won't need them very often, small wrenches such as this one from Equalizer can make difficult jobs easy.

POST-CRASH REPAIRS

When every piece of the helicopter has been accounted for, take them home for cleaning, inspection and repair. Don't attempt field repairs until you're more experienced because there may be damage that isn't immediately obvious. No matter how badly the pieces are broken, take them home with you; it's amazing how parts can be repaired rather easily when they're clean and you're calmer! When you're back in your workshop, disconnect the radio equipment from the helicopter, reattach all the connectors and check for proper operation. Check every servo's movement for smoothness and speed, and listen for unusual noises. If a servo motor runs but the servo output arm doesn't move, a gear inside the case might have been stripped. Having spare gear sets makes this repair easy and inexpensive. More serious malfunctions should be fixed at a radio-repair facility.

Before you can assess the damage accurately, you have to clean the helicopter as well as you can. Use rubbing alcohol and a small stiff brush to remove the dirt and fuel residue, and then wipe the helicopter clean with a cloth. Compressed air from a spray-gun tank is also useful.

Remove the damaged parts, being careful to save all the nuts, bolts, screws and washers in a small container or plastic bag.

Main blades. When the main rotor blades are even slightly damaged, you must be highly cautious. They are heavy and turn at high rpm, and if they come apart while the helicopter is airborne, they can be thrown over a dangerously wide area. In a "tip-over," they're likely to suffer only minor damage that doesn't affect their safe use or their overall performance, especially while you're still training. But if you have even the slightest doubt about their being safe to use, send them back to their manufacturer for a professional inspection and repair.

Tail-rotor blades. Most tail-rotor blades are made of a composite material, so it's easy to see whether they're broken. A common mishap while you're learning is to drag the tail rotor along the ground and scrape the ends of the blades. Minor scrapes shouldn't damage the blades to a point at which they can't be used, and if the scrapes are approximately equal on both blades, you can keep on practicing. If necessary, sand the ends of the blades, and rebalance them when you get home.

Main shaft and axle shaft. Even a minor tip-over can bend the main shaft and/or axle shaft. The axle shaft can be checked quickly by first removing a rotor blade and then turning the axle shaft with a hex driver. While turning it, place your other hand on the rotor head and feel for any movement. Even a slightly bent shaft can be felt as a wobble between a blade grip and the head yoke. If in doubt, remove the shafts and roll them on a table while you look for light between the shaft and the table. A hard table such as that used for a table saw will show even the slightest bends.

If the shaft is slightly bent, you might want to try to straighten it; mark the high side, clamp the shaft in a vise, and hit it with a hammer. To avoid marking the shaft, put a small hardwood block on top of it. It might take a few rounds of banging the shaft and rolling it on the table to check for straightness, but it won't be long before it's almost as good as new.

Don't let a severe crash dismay you because a damaged helicopter always looks worse than it really is, and it will hardly ever be completely destroyed. Once a heli has been repaired and restored to its original condition, it will fly as well as ever.

FORWARD FLIGHT

17

Forward Flight

Before you start to learn forward flight, you should feel pretty confident when hovering. Before you actually start to move the helicopter forward into your first circuit, I'll cover some flight theory, so you'll know what to expect and you'll be ready for problems.

Forward flight with a helicopter is similar to forward flight with an airplane in that similar control responses are needed, and the same principles of aerodynamics apply. If you've flown an RC plane, it will certainly help you to transition to forward flight. So far, you've kept the helicopter very close to you so that you could see even the smallest changes in attitude, and you haven't been overly tasked with the coordination required between bank angle and up-elevator in a turn. You may be able to practice these skills with a simulator or an airplane, if one is available. Perhaps you have a friend who will allow you stick time on his fixed-wing trainer?

Aerodynamically, a helicopter in forward flight is quite similar to an airplane: the rotor disc acts like an airplane wing. It generates lift, not only in a hover but also in forward flight, and this lift is always perpendicular to the rotor plane. For our purposes, this means that the lift is straight up the main shaft. (You'll see the importance of this in a moment.)

Owing to the increased efficiency of the rotor system, the helicopter develops additional

Figure 17-1. Start from forward flight and return to the standard hover position.

lift—translational lift—when it's in forward flight. The rotor system produces more lift in forward flight because of the higher inflow velocity of the air, and this supplies the rotor disc with a greater volume of air per unit of time with which to work than when it's hovering. Translational lift develops with any forward movement, but it depends on airspeed rather than ground speed.

Translational lift can also be present in a hover if there's a wind. This increased efficiency of the rotor system means that the helicopter can maintain forward flight with the same power or less than that required to hover. This will be quite evident when you fly your first circuits because the throttle/collective will be in about the same place as that used for hovering.

Vector analysis can be used to understand how lift is produced by the rotor system. It's important to understand this concept. I don't mean to scare anyone away by talking mathematics, but it's an interesting subject. Refer to

Figure 17-2, which shows a helicopter in a hover. Note that the lift generated goes straight up through the main shaft and exactly counters the weight of the helicopter.

Because the vertical lift equals the weight and there aren't any side forces on the helicopter, it remains in a steady hover. Now let's bank it 30 degrees to the right, as if you were making a turn in your first circuit. In Figure 17-3, notice that the lift is still perpendicular to the rotor disc, but the weight remains straight down because of gravity. Because the lift vector is tilted to the right at an angle of 30 degrees, part of the lift is countering the weight, and part of it is pulling the helicopter to the right. It's this horizontal lift that makes a helicopter, or an airplane, turn. Figure 17-4 is almost the same as Figure 17-3, but now, the total lift of the rotor system is broken down into its two components: the vertical and the horizontal forces of the total lift vector. Notice that since the helicopter was just put into a right bank, the rotor system's lift has not been altered, i.e., its lift still equals that depicted in Figure 17-3. By separating the rotor system's total lift into its two components, we see that the vertical component in Figure 17-3 is now less than the weight. If the lift is less than the weight, the helicopter will obviously descend. But as you fly your first circuit, you certainly don't want to descend whenever you enter a turn, so the answer is to increase the total lift vector (as shown in Figure 17-5) until the vertical component equals the weight. This will again bring the forces (at least, in the vertical plane) to what they were in Figure 17-2. But how do you increase total lift, and how do you know how much lift to add? When the helicopter enters a turn in forward flight, total lift is increased by adding up-elevator (or aft cyclic) to increase the angle of attack of the rotor disc. How much you increase lift or how much up-elevator you apply will depend on the helicopter's flight performance and on the angle of bank. If you apply too much up-elevator, the helicopter will climb and, obviously, too little up-elevator will cause it to descend.

Another important consideration is that the up-elevator needed to maintain level flight in a coordinated turn will depend on the helicopter's angle of bank. In Figure 17-6, notice that now, the angle of bank has been increased to 60 degrees. That doesn't leave much vertical lift to counter the weight. For further illustration, look at Figure 17-7, which shows the helicopter in a 90-degree bank. As you can see, there's no vertical component in the total lift vector, so no matter how much up-elevator you apply, there won't be any lift to counter the weight, and the helicopter will,

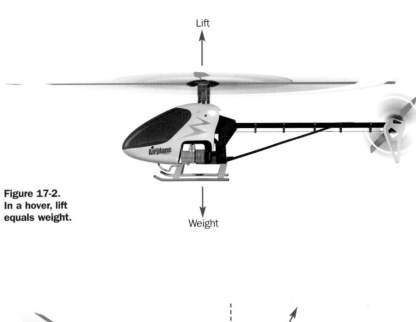

Figure 17-2. In a hover, lift equals weight.

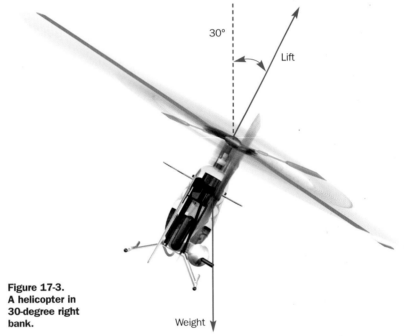

Figure 17-3. A helicopter in 30-degree right bank.

therefore, lose altitude. Figure 17-8 shows the helicopter with an angle of bank greater than 90 degrees, and here, any up-elevator will produce lift, but now, the lift vector is in the wrong direction—downward—and that is added to the weight vector. There are times when you want this, e.g., during the second half of a loop, a split-S, or any other vertical maneuver in which the nose is low. From this simple explanation, I think you'll

realize that angle of bank is very important to your first circuits; when the angle of bank increases, you need more coordinated up-elevator to maintain level flight.

The last theoretical point to consider before you try forward flight: does your main rotor turn clockwise or counterclockwise? I described the rotor system's torque and its effects on the helicopter in an earlier chapter, but these factors are important here,

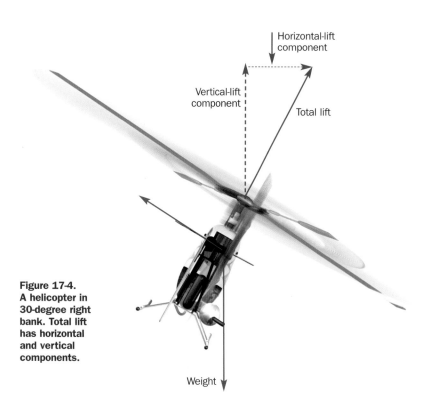

**Figure 17-4.
A helicopter in
30-degree right
bank. Total lift
has horizontal
and vertical
components.**

Horizontal-lift
component

Vertical-lift
component

Total lift

Weight

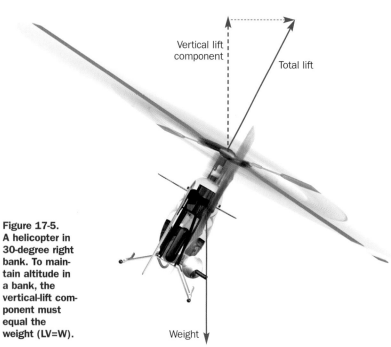

**Figure 17-5.
A helicopter in
30-degree right
bank. To main-
tain altitude in
a bank, the
vertical-lift com-
ponent must
equal the
weight (LV=W).**

Vertical lift
component

Total lift

Weight

too. A helicopter with a clockwise-rotating rotor system will turn more easily to the right, and a helicopter with a counterclockwise system will turn more easily to the left. I therefore recommend that you plan to fly the circuit in the direction in which the helicopter will turn most easily because flying it in that direction will require very little, if any, coordination of the tail rotor.

ADVANCE TO FORWARD FLIGHT

It's difficult to determine accurately when it will be time for you to advance to forward flight. Some progress rapidly and have lots of confidence but then start forward flying too soon and damage their helicopters. On the other hand, I've seen many who have really good control of their helicopters who want to be even more proficient before they take the plunge. Only you can decide. As a rule, if you can comfortably fly figure-8s in front of you, and your control of the helicopter is more or less second nature and doesn't require all your attention and effort, you're probably ready to move on to forward flight. It isn't really difficult, but it's the first time you'll have your helicopter well away from the ground.

Before you fly forward in your first circuit, you need to make some mechanical changes to your helicopter. When you first set up the helicopter, you adjusted the collective and cyclic settings for learning how to hover. Now that you're more in control of the helicopter and need more control movement, you need to make some changes in the control setup.

If you've left the cyclic sensitivity set to half movement for full-stick throw, you may not have enough control to fly your first circuit. Therefore, increase the cyclic throw so that ¾ swashplate throw is available with full control-stick movement. This change will, of course, depend on your particular helicopter and your personal "feel," but it's something you should consider. Evaluate the helicopter's response as you fly figure-8s in front of you. Do you have enough control to maneuver the helicopter briskly without full stick deflection? You should always have some reserve control movement in case things go wrong and you have to make a recovery. But this must also be weighed against having an overly sensitive helicopter. As a rule, it's easier to control a sensitive aileron setting than an oversensitive elevator.

When we set up the helicopter for hovering, the collective was initially limited in throw to between 0 and 5 degrees.

But for forward flight and to descend for landing, this setting won't provide enough collective control. You should increase the collective top end to approximately 7 degrees; this will give you a reserve in collective to enable the helicopter to climb, but it isn't so much collective that it will overload the engine and cause it to die in flight. I hope you won't need full power and collective (at least, for your first few circuits), but it's nice to know it's there if you need it.

For the minimum collective setting, I recommend about -2 degrees instead of the previous setting of 0. This enables the helicopter to descend without significantly reducing its rotor speed. If you don't let the blades go to a negative collective-pitch setting, the helicopter may not descend, or it might descend very slowly and with reduced rotor rpm. This might not seem so bad, but just as you have extra collec-

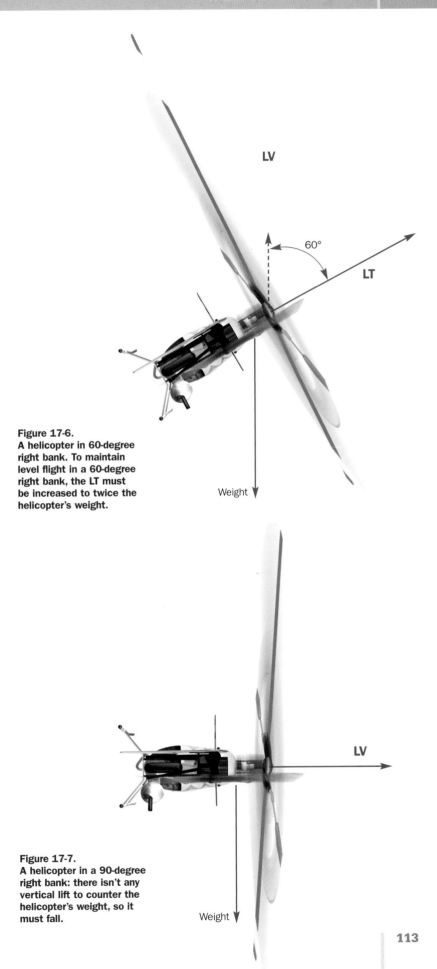

Figure 17-6.
A helicopter in 60-degree right bank. To maintain level flight in a 60-degree right bank, the LT must be increased to twice the helicopter's weight.

Figure 17-7.
A helicopter in a 90-degree right bank: there isn't any vertical lift to counter the helicopter's weight, so it must fall.

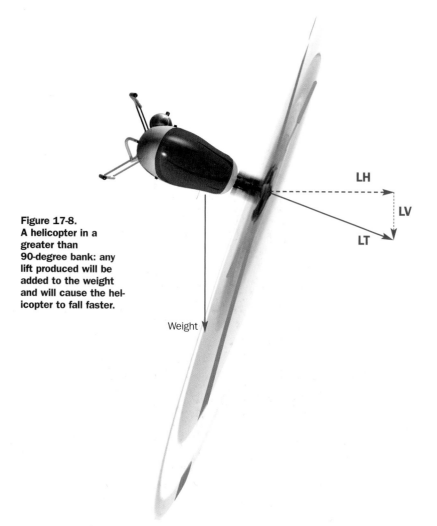

Figure 17-8.
A helicopter in a greater than 90-degree bank: any lift produced will be added to the weight and will cause the helicopter to fall faster.

LH

LV

LT

Weight

midpoint position. When the stick is advanced, the radio must assume it's climbing. On some of the more advanced radios, if you like to hover with the throttle stick elsewhere than in the midpoint position, you can tell the radio when you're hovering by bringing the helicopter into a hover and then turning on the hover-memory switch. This tells the radio that you're in a hover and that it should apply the compensations from that stick position.

As for the second part of the question—how much compensation to provide—it will depend on your helicopter. First, make sure that the tail-rotor compensation is turned on and set either to a clockwise or a counterclockwise rotation, depending on your helicopter. These two switches are usually under the transmitter cover among the many adjustments, or in a program on a computer radio. Somewhere on the transmitter, there are usually one or two knobs to set the amount of tail-rotor compensation. If you have only one knob, the compensation amount will be the same when the helicopter is climbing or descending, but in opposite directions. If your radio has two knobs, they should be marked "Up" and "Down." For your initial circuits, set the knob(s)—or your computer program—to their midrange positions and adjust them more finely later as needed.

Helicopter radios also have an "idle-up" function. This is really nothing more than a governor that restricts the engine's minimum speed. But before we get into setting it, let's look again at why we need it. This is useful when landing because even though the collective is reduced almost to its minimum setting to allow the helicopter to descend in

tive to help you climb if you need to, so should you have extra collective in the negative direction to facilitate a more rapid descent when needed.

The two other controls—the throttle and the tail rotor—can be left where they are. You should also make other changes to your transmitter, if it's designed for helicopters.

One of the reasons you bought a helicopter radio was to gain more control over the helicopter, but until now, you didn't need these extra features. If you are not using a heading-hold gyro, you'll find your radio's tail-rotor compensation system convenient. I described this in the chapter on radios, but I'll review it here. Basically, this feature adds a little

tail-rotor input when you climb, and it takes out a little tail rotor when you descend. Starting with the helicopter in a hover, when you add power/collective to climb, the torque balance is disturbed, and an increase in torque is seen on the helicopter because of the increase in pitch of the blades. On a clockwise-rotating rotor system, this increase in torque moves the nose to the left, and the compensating system automatically adds a little right tail rotor. But how does the radio know when the helicopter is climbing and how much compensation it should add? To answer the first part of the question: the radio assumes that the helicopter is in a hover when the throttle/collective stick is in its forward flight, the throttle is kept open at a preset setting to maintain rotor rpm. If the idle-up isn't used and the throttle is reduced to near idle, not only will the helicopter descend, but the main- and tail-rotor speed will also be reduced. This reduction in rotor speed will make the helicopter more difficult to control; it could greatly increase its rate of descent; and it will also require a greater transition back to hover. With the idle-up properly set, however, there should be hardly any change in rotor speed throughout the landing pattern, from normal forward flight and back to a hover.

Refer to your radio's instruction manual to adjust your specific idle-up. Many radios have a graph or a numeric display to show the relationship of the stick position to the throttle position. A good initial adjustment of the idle-up is to have 30-percent throttle at idle, 50-percent throttle at half stick and 40 percent in between. These are just initial settings that you'll adjust later to suit your particular engine and helicopter.

Now that you've made all these changes, refuel and get used to these new settings. If the helicopter feels too sensitive or not sensitive enough, adjust the cyclic throws and/or dual rates. Also be careful of the collective because you now have the capability to climb and descend rapidly, and this will also make the stick more sensitive. You'll notice while hovering, or even while flying a figure-8 pattern in front of you, that the tail-rotor compensation has little, if any, effect. This is usual because you're still maneuvering at close to the hover collective setting, and it isn't a cause for concern.

As you practice using the idle-up, be careful not to switch it on with a low rotor speed. This would cause the throttle and, therefore, the rotor speed, to increase rapidly, and it could strain the drive system. I prefer to increase the throttle almost to the hover setting and then turn on the idle-up, which doesn't change the helicopter's performance. I also wait to turn off the idle-up until I've just landed and the rotor speed is still fairly high, as this then lets me decrease the rotor speed slowly for a more scale-like appearance. It will take a little practice to get used to the idle-up, and you should be able to switch it on and off without ever looking at the transmitter. Perhaps sliding a little piece of fuel tubing over the switch will make it easier to find when you need it.

Practice hovering and flying the figure-8 pattern with these new settings until you feel comfortable. Some of you will take only a tank or two of fuel to achieve this; others may want a few more practice sessions on these new settings. But please don't move on to the next step until you're sure that you're ready.

Now that you've completely adjusted the helicopter and practiced enough with it, there are two basic ways to move on to forward flight: the first is what I call the "fly-around": you stand in the center of a circle and fly the helicopter around you, moving it progressively farther away until it's well away from you. The second technique is progressing straight to the "normal circuit": fly away while climbing and turning to the downwind and then back to final. This is the classic approach for a helicopter and an airplane, and it's the basic pattern you'll eventually fly. Either approach will work well to get you into and out of forward flight, so the choice is up to you; I discuss them both.

It seems as though, just as we're ready to take the plunge into forward flight, there are always more points I must mention.

First, I recommend that you choose a sunny, fairly calm day to try your first forward flights. The sun will make the helicopter easier to see as it gets away from you, and a relatively light wind will keep its ground speed down to something reasonable as you turn downwind. I don't think it's a good idea to practice in the early morning or evening because the sun is near the horizon and could blind you somewhere in the pattern. Flying when the sun is high could prevent this from happening. (Wear a hat and sunglasses.)

THE FLY-AROUND
Assuming that your helicopter has a clockwise-rotating main rotor system, start from the usual hover position with the helicopter to your left and about 20 feet in front of you, facing into any breeze there might be (no more than a light breeze). Just as you've already practiced flying figure-8s, start in the same way but now continue, very slowly, to fly to the right. If your helicopter has a counterclockwise main rotor system, everything is the same, but all the turns will be to the left instead of to the right. You'll notice that very little, if any, tail-rotor coordination is required, and forward speed is controlled by the pitch attitude of the nose.

To increase the forward speed, just drop the nose slightly, and to slow down, raise the nose slightly. Also be careful not to get the helicopter completely broadside to you; it's a position you haven't seen before, and it's easy to become confused about which control input to make as a correction.

When you've flown a complete circle, bring the helicopter back to a hover and then land, bringing the engine back to idle. How did it

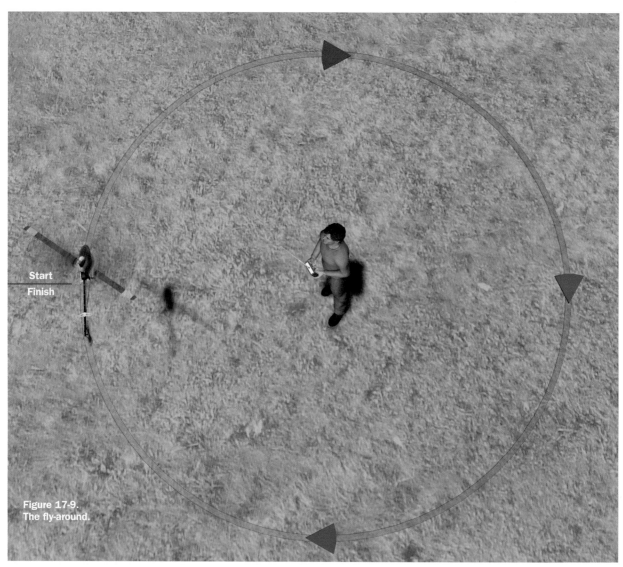

**Start
Finish**

Figure 17-9.
The fly-around.

go? What were your mistakes? Did you always look at the nose during the flight? I didn't mention idle-up or tail-rotor compensation for this phase of training because the helicopter is basically in a hover. When you again feel comfortable and have realized what you need to correct in future flights, try again. Soon, you'll feel very confident in this small circle, and then it will be time to fly bigger and bigger circles and farther away from the ground. When your circles are fairly large, you can roll out to level flight for a short time, e.g., on the downward or final, and transition into the more classic pattern described in the next section.

THE NORMAL CIRCUIT

You'll need good weather again, but for the normal circuit, a breeze of 5 to 10mph will help you to keep the nose straight while on final during takeoffs and landings. It will also slow the helicopter's ground speed as you take off and land.

Refer to Figure 17-10 for an illustration of the basic circuit. As you increase the throttle almost to the hover setting, turn on the idle-up switch. Then, with the helicopter again in the normal hover position in front and to the left of you, add only a little power/collective and lower the nose slightly. This will enable the helicopter to climb slightly and

start flying forward. Again, control the forward speed by using the pitch attitude of the nose, and control the rate of climb with the collective. When the helicopter gets 30 to 50 feet in front of the hover position, bank the helicopter slightly to the right using right cyclic, and continue a climbing turn to point A, at which you'll need left cyclic to roll out to level flight. Remember to keep the angle of bank fairly shallow—30 degrees or less. You'll also need to apply up-elevator during the turn to move the nose around, just as you did when flying figure-8s, and you'll probably be able to make a nice turn without needing any coordinated tail rotor. The heli-

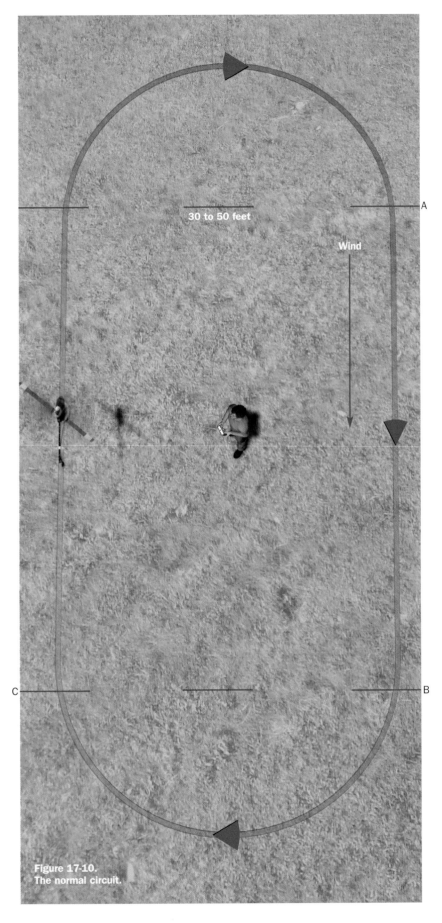

30 to 50 feet

Wind

A

C

B

**Figure 17-10.
The normal circuit.**

copter should now be at an altitude of 25 to 50 feet, going downwind at a reasonable speed and with the power reduced to about what you used for hovering. You can control altitude using the helicopter's pitch attitude and forward speed, and you'll need to properly coordinate collective for a smooth, slow flight at a constant altitude. Continue to turn with the helicopter to keep it in front and to the left of you, as this is a comfortable position.

I emphasize the importance of keeping the helicopter moving forward until it's safely in front of you in the normal hover position. If, during the circuit or at any other time, you fail to keep the helicopter flying forward, you'll be in a hover or flying backwards; there aren't any other options. If you let the helicopter hover in an unusual position, it will be affected by wind forces of which you may not be aware, and you won't be able to see the changes in helicopter position quickly enough to make the required control inputs. This will not only make the helicopter move, but also the control inputs won't have the same effect as they do in a hover. Also, if the helicopter is actually backing up, maintaining directional control without the aid of a heading-hold gyro is extremely difficult because the big vertical fin doesn't like to go first; it likes to follow. The nose may therefore swing around abruptly and further disorient you.

When the helicopter gets to point B, about 50 to 100 feet away from you, again use cyclic and up-elevator to start a right turn to point C. Keep the bank fairly shallow and coordinate with up-elevator. Too much up-elevator will start the helicopter climbing, but insufficient elevator will allow it to descend. The tail should also follow the nose and should not skid through the turn. Coordinate with tail rotor, if required.

To get used to seeing the helicopter in forward flight and to get used to the coordination required in the turns, fly several of these circuits at an altitude of about 50 feet. As long as you have plenty of fuel, don't be in too much of a hurry to land; just relax, practice, and build your confidence.

When you're ready to try your first landing approach, take the helicopter to point C and keep it in forward flight as you decrease the throttle/collective to start it descending. Again, control its forward speed with pitch attitude and its rate of descent with collective. The helicopter should not stop its forward flight until it's back to its usual hover position.

As the helicopter passes well to your left, begin to raise the nose slightly to stop its forward flight, and transition back to the usual hover position. As the helicopter stops, advance the power to that required for hover, but the idle-up should keep the rotor speed fairly constant. Once in a hover, bring the helicopter back to the ground, but switch off the idle-up before you reduce the throttle to idle, and continue to maintain control of the helicopter as the rotor speed decreases.

The idle-up function should have maintained the rotor speed while the helicopter was descending. If the rotor speed increased during descent, reduce the idle-up and vice versa. Again, it will take a few approaches to get the adjustment just right.

Now that I've described how to progress to forward flight, I'll discuss some of the "not recommended" techniques that I've seen people using. The first is the "forward flight and stop." The pilot goes from a hover into slow forward flight at hover altitude until the helicopter is 50 to 100 feet in front of him. Then he tries to stop the helicopter and fly backwards to the original position. This has several disadvantages, and it could lead to a crash. First, the helicopter is difficult to see (and, therefore, to control) when it's that far in front of you in a hover. You can't see the small changes in the helicopter that require control corrections, and you may therefore lose control altogether.

Also, with the helicopter that close to the ground, there isn't much room for mistakes, and that altitude could be lost rather quickly. Last, and perhaps most important, is that the helicopter must be hovered backwards to its original position. Hovering backwards (without a heading-hold gyro), especially when there's hardly any wind, could cause the tail to swing around violently because it acts like feathers on an arrow to keep the nose going first. This requires a lot of tail-rotor coordination that you haven't had to use before, and it's easy to make a mistake. This happened to me when I was learning because I thought I was better than I really was. The nose swung very quickly, and it either continued to turn or I put in the wrong control input, but it came over my head spinning very quickly and hit the ground almost upside-down, causing a great deal of damage. I hope this won't happen to you.

Another poor technique is the "high climb." This is when the helicopter goes straight up from its normal hover position to an altitude of 50 feet or more, and the pilot tries to descend into a hover. This again puts the helicopter in a completely different attitude than what you're used to seeing, and it's rather difficult to see it and stay oriented with it when it's that high. Another problem is that, during the descent, the helicopter could descend in its own rotor wash, thereby reducing the rotor blades' effective lift and causing an increased, and possibly uncontrolled, descent. There really isn't much to be gained from this sort of practice, and because no attempt was made to fly forward, the helicopter was basically in a hover all the time and just climbing and descending. Remember, the helicopter doesn't know how much air is beneath it.

When you've landed, always think about your circuit and possibly make notes to read later at home. Only by analyzing our flights can we hope to improve and avoid repeating our mistakes.

Pre-Aerobatics

Now that you feel confident when hovering and flying circuits, you'll be eager to attempt more advanced aerobatic maneuvers. I'll get into some of them in the next chapter, but right now, it's very important that you learn two pre-aerobatic maneuvers: the nose-in hover and autorotation. Although I don't think a nose-in hover is really a maneuver, I'll refer to it as such because it's important for you to feel comfortable maneuvering the helicopter in all flying positions. Autorotation is an emergency, engine-out descent to a safe landing without damaging the helicopter. No matter how reliable your engine, there's always a chance that it may fail, or that you may run out of fuel, burn out a glow plug, etc. The chance of an engine's failing is also increased when you do aerobatics because it's running at close to maximum power, it's using a lot of fuel, and it's straining itself to its limits. I'm not saying that the engine and the other equipment aren't made to withstand this sort of use, but aerobatic flying does present more risk of component failure.

NOSE-IN HOVER

Figure 18-1. This is hovering the helicopter with the nose facing you. Perfecting this type of flying requires the same type of dedication as you practiced while learning to hover, i.e., you must really concentrate on the helicopter movements and the required control inputs.

Some controls are the same whether you're behind the helicopter or facing it; one such control is collective. Adding collective will make the helicopter gain altitude and, by now, you should have a good feel for the collective required to maintain a good hover. If you've changed the collective settings for forward flight, these settings should also be good for practicing nose-in hovering. Be careful that they aren't too sensitive because collective control should be a given by now, and a control that's too sensitive could result in some rather hard landings during practice.

The other control that remains the same is the tail rotor. That may not seem right because usually, a right tail-rotor command makes the nose move to the right, but now, with the nose facing you, a right tail-rotor command will make the nose move to the left. That's certainly true, but rather than think of the nose moving from one side to the other, think of it as moving clockwise or counterclockwise. A right tail-rotor command really makes the helicopter's nose move in a clockwise direction, and that remains the same whether the

nose is facing you or not. I don't recommend that you look at other parts of the helicopter instead of the nose while you practice this maneuver. I've heard of people looking at the tail while the nose is facing them: the tail-rotor command will still move the tail in the same direction as the stick is moved. This is a very bad technique because you should always be looking at the helicopter's nose while flying in any direction.

The rest of the controls—right/left and fore/aft cyclic—are the ones that are reversed, and they deserve most of your attention while you practice. When the nose faces you, a right-cyclic command will make the helicopter move to your left (Figure 18-1) and vice versa. In the same way, an aft-cyclic command will raise the nose and cause the helicopter to hover backwards.

There are three basic training techniques to learn how to nose-in hover, and I'll leave it to you to decide which you like best.

1. From the ground up
This technique involves putting the training gear back on your helicopter so that you can prac-

Figure 18-1. Nose-in hovering. Looking at the nose, a right-cyclic command on the transmitter moves the swash-plate and helicopter to your left.

tice without ever getting the helicopter very far off the ground. The advantages of this technique are that the helicopter is close to the ground, so it's unlikely to be damaged if you make a mistake; and you'll get the most out of each session because the helicopter is always facing you. It's important that the helicopter be fairly close to you because you must be able to see its movements and the required corrections. The only real disadvantage of this technique is that you have to use training gear, and this prohibits other types of flying.

With a full tank of fuel and the training gear strapped to your helicopter, pick a flat area on which to practice, and place the helicopter on the ground and facing into the wind. With your back to the wind, stand about 15 feet in front and slightly to the side of the helicopter so that you're looking at the nose. This is important: the helicopter should always be facing into the wind so that the vertical fin will help to keep the nose steady, thereby giving you more opportunity to practice with the cyclic controls.

As you add power/collective, continue to look at, and fly, the helicopter's nose. Use your peripheral vision to assess the position of the tail boom and training gear, which will give you a good, level-hover indication. At this stage, never let the helicopter get more than 6 to 12 inches off the ground, and take frequent breaks to analyze your mistakes.

2. The high approach
This technique for practicing the nose-in hover gets the helicopter well away from the ground so that you'll be able to recover the helicopter safely into forward flight if you make a mistake. In this case, altitude is your friend; it

gives you time to make a recovery, and it also gets you away from the training gear and lets you fly circuits when you're tired of practicing. The three disadvantages of this technique are:

• It assumes that when you make a mistake while practicing, you'll be able to recover the helicopter before it crashes.

• Time and fuel are wasted while you fly around trying to get into the "high position."

• The practice hover position is quite high and puts the helicopter in an unfamiliar position. Slight changes in helicopter attitude may be difficult to detect and, therefore, to correct.

To try this technique, set up the helicopter as desired for normal forward flight, but if possible, slightly desensitize the cyclic controls to avoid over-controlling. Fly a normal circuit, and as the helicopter approaches you at an altitude of 30 feet or so, with your

back to the wind, slow its forward speed slightly, and move the cyclic controls to get a feel for their reaction as the helicopter flies towards you. During the following circuits, while looking at the nose, continue to slow the helicopter more and more as you increasingly gain a feel for its controls. Eventually, you'll reach a point at which the helicopter is in a hover at an altitude of about 30 feet and about 30 feet in front of you.

If, at any time during this process, you lose orientation with the helicopter, lower the nose and turn the machine away from you to transition into forward flight away from you. Also, be careful not to reduce the collective. Remember, in this case, altitude is your friend, and the collective will keep the helicopter away from the ground.

3. The walk-around
This third technique starts with the helicopter in a normal hover position with you facing the rear quarter. Keep the helicopter facing into the wind, and slowly walk

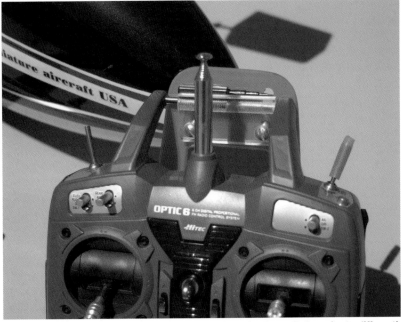

A piece of fuel tubing on an important switch will make the switch easier to differentiate from the others while you're flying.

around towards the nose to sort of "sneak up on" nose-in hovering. The advantage of this technique is that the helicopter is again set up for normal hovering and flight, and you start from a comfortable position behind it. You can also practice looking at the side and front quarter as well as at the nose. The disadvantage here is that the helicopter is close to the ground, and this doesn't give you a lot of time to recover if you make a mistake.

Begin by putting the helicopter into the normal hover position about 5 or 6 feet high. While keeping it stationary and facing into the wind, continue to face it as you slowly walk around to its side. Don't get too close to it during this stage, and be mindful of the direction in which you need to move the cyclic control stick to keep the helicopter away from you if you become disoriented. When you feel comfortable in this position, slowly move around towards the nose (always facing the helicopter) until you can hover while looking at the nose.

To recover from a mistake, turn the nose away from you with the tail rotor, and transition either back into a normal hover or into forward flight away from you. Again, do not reduce the collective. You may even have to add it quickly to transition into a climb because you'll need to keep the helicopter well away from the ground.

ADVANCED NOSE-IN HOVERING

When you feel comfortable looking at the nose, it's time to move the helicopter slightly back and forth in a figure-8 maneuver to feel comfortable controlling it in forward flight as the nose faces you. Begin from the nose-in hover position with the helicopter about 10 feet high and 20 feet in front

of you. With cyclic commands, move the helicopter right and left slowly, just to get used to its moving from one position to another. As you progressively feel more comfortable looking at the nose, move the helicopter not only with cyclic commands but also by coordinating the tail rotor to turn the nose in the direction of flight. With just a little practice, you'll be doing figure-8s in front of you while looking only at the nose.

Another variation on this maneuver is the rearward climb. With the helicopter hovering nose in, add a little power/collective to start a climb, but also coordinate with aft cyclic to enable the helicopter to climb as it backs away from you. You'll need just a little aft cyclic, but you might need more tail rotor in the direction of blade rotation to counteract the large increase in torque. Also be careful not to back up faster than the wind is blowing, or the vertical fin will swing the helicopter around to keep the nose facing into the wind.

When you've reached this stage of flying, you should really feel good about the control you have over the helicopter, no matter in which direction it's facing. Because you now have the skill and confidence to recover the helicopter from any position, you can progress to aerobatics.

AUTOROTATIONS

I mentioned previously the need to be proficient in autorotation landings to cope with landing with engine failure, but an autorotation is, in itself, also a very demanding maneuver, and it's a challenge to execute correctly. To practice autorotations, you won't need to change the sensitivity or throw of the cyclic controls or the tail rotor, but you must make some adjustments to the collective-pitch range, and you'll have

to adjust your helicopter radio's throttle-hold function.

Until now, the collective range has been adjusted to provide a maximum collective setting that allows the helicopter to climb enough without overloading the engine, while the minimum collective setting provides an adequate rate of descent with the idle-up selected to maintain rotor rpm. Typical values for this collective range are in the order of -2 degrees to about 10 degrees. This collective range is not suitable for autorotations for the following reasons:

• The minimum collective setting of -2 degrees won't allow the helicopter to descend fast enough to maintain or increase the rotor rpm. During an autorotation, the collective must be reduced to a setting that will allow the uprush of air to keep the rotor blades spinning at a high speed, and this kinetic energy stored in the rotor blades is converted into lift as the collective pitch is increased during the flare and landing.

• The maximum collective setting of about 8 degrees will provide a certain amount of lift during the flare and landing, but much greater lift can be obtained by increasing the collective pitch to 12 to 14 degrees, if possible. This increase in collective pitch will give a much softer landing and will also provide an extra safety margin if the collective isn't perfectly coordinated during landing.

Before you make any adjustments to your radio, refer to the owners' manual to review your particular radio's features in the throttle-hold mode of operation. All helicopter radios will allow the throttle-hold function to be adjusted somewhere on the radio. This function is used to

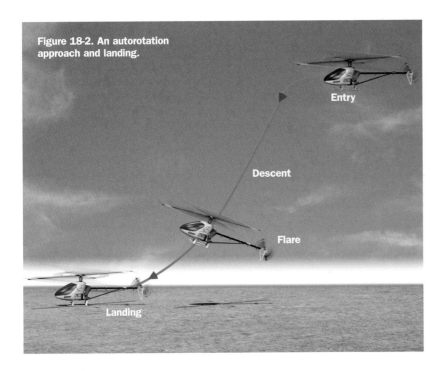

Figure 18-2. An autorotation approach and landing.

Entry

Descent

Flare

Landing

first autorotations. Pick a clear day on which you'll be able to stay oriented with the helicopter when it's flying fairly high. A slight, steady breeze of 5 to 10mph is ideal because it will provide translational lift throughout touchdown, and this, in turn, will reduce the amount of collective required.

Before you try your first autorotation, it's important to understand the sequence of events, the principles involved and the required control movements and coordination. Begin by reviewing the autorotation approach and landing as shown in Figure 18-2. Notice that it's composed of three distinct stages: the entry, the descent and the flare/landing.

THE ENTRY

For initial entry practice, have the helicopter at an altitude of about 100 feet in slow forward flight into the wind with the idle-up turned off and slightly downwind of you (Figure 18-3). This will allow the helicopter to descend at about a 45-degree angle in slow forward flight past you, so you'll be looking at the helicopter's rear quarter during

bring the engine back to a nearly idle condition during flight to simulate an engine-out condition, but it also allows you to advance the throttle, if needed, by turning off the throttle-hold mode.

Most helicopter radios also offer a separate collective-pitch range in the throttle-hold mode. This is a very desirable feature because it enables you to operate in the pitch range of -2 degrees to 10 degrees for normal flying but changes the collective throw automatically to increased values for autorotations. Read your owners' manual, and make the adjustments necessary to obtain a pitch range of -3 degrees to 12 degrees in the throttle-hold mode while still retaining your normal pitch range for other flight modes.

Initially, you should set the throttle position in the throttle-hold mode with the engine off. This is important because the throttle-hold position may be grossly out of adjustment, and if the throttle-hold switch was turned on with the engine running, it could suddenly increase

to a high power setting. Therefore, adjust the throttle so it's in the same position as when the throttle stick is in the full slow position and the engine trim is at its maximum position. Because the engine will idle safely with the throttle in this position, the throttle-hold function should give a good steady idle as well.

With these preliminary adjustments made on the workbench, you're now ready to practice your

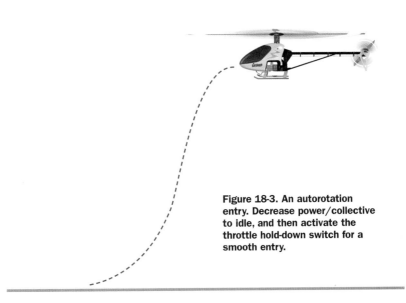

Figure 18-3. An autorotation entry. Decrease power/collective to idle, and then activate the throttle hold-down switch for a smooth entry.

the flare and touchdown. When the helicopter reaches this entry position, smoothly reduce the throttle/collective to the full idle position without turning on the throttle-hold function, and just see how the helicopter descends. Hold the nose fairly level to prevent the helicopter from descending too rapidly, and make sure that the idle trim is in the full fast position to ensure that the engine doesn't quit.

THE DESCENT

During the descent, the helicopter's pitch attitude will control both the rate of descent and the amount of forward movement—possibly even more than the blades' negative pitch does (Figure 18-4). Initially, strive to maintain a rate of descent that's reasonable and controllable but not so slow as to reduce the rotor blades' speed. During the descent, notice also that you must look at the helicopter's nose—another good reason to have this mastered before you attempt other advanced maneuvers.

When the helicopter has lost about half of its altitude, increase the throttle/collective and transition to forward flight. That's enough practice for the first attempt. Fly around, put the

helicopter in the entry position again, and reduce the power to idle without using the throttle-hold function. This time, vary the helicopter's pitch attitude slightly during the descent and notice the large effect this has on the descent rate. It will take only a slight nose-down pitch attitude to make the descent uncomfortably fast. Continue to practice in this way until you feel comfortable entering and descending under control.

Before you progress to the next stage of autorotations, check that the throttle-hold engine setting is set to a very fast idle. At this setting, on the ground, the rotor blades should turn fairly fast but not fast enough to allow a hover. Now, again enter the autorotation as already described, but flip the throttle-hold switch. This increased engine-idle speed should not have any effect on the rotor blades' rpm because they'll be turning quite a bit faster than the engine speed will allow. You may, however, notice a slight increase in the helicopter's rate of descent because the negative pitch has now been increased. Again, when the helicopter has lost about half of its altitude and with the throttle in the full low position, turn off the throttle-

hold function, and advance the throttle to transition to forward flight. Continue to practice in this way to get used to switching the throttle hold on and off as needed and to evaluate the rate of descent with that particular negative-pitch setting. To make the autorotation controllable while maintaining rotor speed, readjust the negative pitch as needed to increase or decrease the rate of descent. Actually, maintaining rotor speed shouldn't be a problem with the engine set at a very fast idle, but it must always be considered.

THE FLARE & LANDING

When you feel comfortable with the entry and descent with the engine still set at a high idle, it's time to try the flare and landing (Figure 18-5). The high idle speed will be helpful during this phase of the maneuver because it will prevent the rotor speed from decaying too rapidly but will still allow a touchdown.

The flare and touchdown are harder to do on a calm day because of the lack of translational lift. They are also more difficult to do from a more vertical descent. As an example, consider the helicopter in a vertical descent in position A (Figure 18-6). When the helicopter reaches position B, the reduction in its rate of descent must begin, but the only way to do this is to increase the collective. Typically, you should start this increase in collective at a higher altitude; more drag is placed on the rotor system, and the rotor speed is therefore decreased. This decrease in rotor speed will also cause the helicopter to descend even faster, but you can counter that with more collective to further slow the rate of descent. As you can probably see, you must, therefore, increase the collective in a way that reduces the rate of descent enough to provide a soft

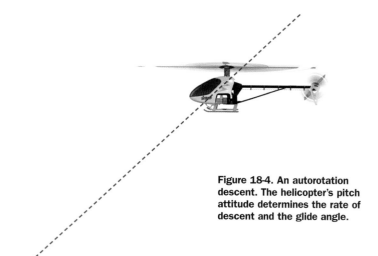

Figure 18-4. An autorotation descent. The helicopter's pitch attitude determines the rate of descent and the glide angle.

Figure 18-5. An autorotation flare and landing. The flare stops the helicopter's forward speed and increases the rotor system's lift. During a landing, the helicopter is brought to a level attitude, and collective pitch is increased for a gentle touchdown.

landing while still maintaining rotor rpm. If you've added too much collective by the time the helicopter reaches point C (or you increased collective too soon), the helicopter won't have enough rotor speed to provide enough lift for a soft landing. On the other hand, if you haven't added enough collective by point C, the helicopter will have a fast rate of descent and a hard landing. By now, I think you're beginning to get the idea that the point at which you increase collective and the rate at which you increase it throughout the flare and touchdown are especially critical in this more vertical descent.

Now let's look at how we may make this flare and touchdown coordination a little easier. Refer to Figure 18-7, and note that again, the helicopter is in an autorotation mode, but this time, with a slight forward velocity into the wind. As the helicopter passes point A at an altitude of about 15 feet, which is the same position as in Figure 18-6; no further action is required, and the helicopter can be allowed to continue its descent. Review Figure 18-7: as the helicop-

ter reaches point B, its forward velocity across the ground must be reduced, or it will land much like an airplane. To reduce and eventually stop the forward motion, raise the nose slightly. During this time, the helicopter has descended further to point C. Some very important aspects of this maneuver between points B and C may not be readily apparent:

• The forward velocity has been eliminated.

• The collective has been maintained in its full negative position.

• The rotor speed has remained high or has even increased.

• The helicopter has been descending, but it is moving more slowly because of the increased lift on the rotor system caused by the increase in the entire rotor disc's angle of attack.

• At point C, the helicopter is only about 2 feet off the ground.

Now that you've arrived at position C, you must bring the helicopter's pitch angle back to level flight with forward cyclic. As you can imagine, timing is again very important. If you bring the helicopter back to level flight too soon, it will still be moving forward; if you do it too late, it will be moving backwards—a very dangerous position.

Also, as you push the elevator forward to level the helicopter, you also reduce the entire rotor system's angle of attack and, therefore, you reduce overall lift. You compensated for this by increasing the collective and again trading rotor speed for altitude and a soft touchdown. In this case, notice that collective only needs to be coordinated from an altitude of 2 feet and not the 15 feet given in the previous example. This is what makes an autorotation landing from forward flight so much easier to do. And while you push the nose forward to level flight and coordinate an increase in collective, the helicopter advances to position D and is just several inches off the ground. But be careful here and throughout touchdown: because of the large

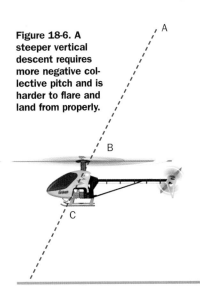

Figure 18-6. A steeper vertical descent requires more negative collective pitch and is harder to flare and land from properly.

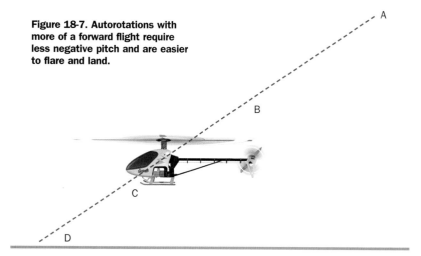

Figure 18-7. Autorotations with more of a forward flight require less negative pitch and are easier to flare and land.

increase in torque produced by the increase in collective, the helicopter will attempt to yaw in the opposite direction as blade rotation. You must compensate for this with the tail rotor. Then, to produce a soft landing, you have only to continually increase collective as the rotor speed decays. When you feel comfortable doing autos at this higher throttle-hold setting, continue to practice, decreasing the engine speed little by little until you have the engine all the way to idle.

As you become proficient in autorotation approaches and landings, you should still make the entry by completely reducing the throttle/collective before you flip the throttle-hold switch on. This will ensure a smooth transition to the descent phase. If you activated the throttle-hold switch from level flight, the helicopter would lose power abruptly and yaw as the torque changed, causing a very sloppy entry. I always like to end my flights with a real autorotation landing, i.e., I bring the engine trim back to full low so that the engine quits as I reduce the throttle to idle. When you make the helicopter descend with its tail rotor stopped and no sound other than that of the rotor blades swooshing through the air, you'll always impress the crowd!

You should practice autos on a windy day—say 10 to 20mph winds—because it offers the advantage of providing translational lift during the flare and touchdown, and it makes it almost impossible to overshoot your landing spot because the wind prevents the helicopter from going too far upwind. On a calm day, however, losing translational lift and overshooting your landing spot can be real problems.

On a calm day, you'll have to make a shallower final approach and keep the helicopter in forward flight until it's close to the ground. If you come down more in the vertical with little forward flight speed, you'll need to add collective at a much higher altitude, and you'll risk losing all your lift at a higher altitude. Doing autos on a calm day is much harder than doing them on a windy day, so the first time you try these, I suggest that you increase the throttle-hold engine speed again to provide a little reserve during the flare and landing.

Calm-day autos can also result in your overshooting your landing spot and landing well away from your usual area. When people see that they're about to overshoot, they commonly tend to slow the forward flight speed by raising the nose. Well, that's what we usually

do under powered flight, so shouldn't it work here also? Unfortunately, the answer is no. Raising the nose to slow down will result in a dramatic reduction in rotor speed and will put you well away from the ground with little reserve rotor speed for the flare and landing.

If you're ever about to overshoot, simply abort the maneuver and continue to fly the helicopter under power. For some reason, when in throttle hold, many seem to think they've committed themselves to landing, but if it doesn't look good, bail out.

As you make progress with autorotations, experiment with different pitch settings to optimize your particular helicopter's performance. If -3 degrees doesn't get you down quickly enough on a calm day and causes you to overshoot, try -4 or -5 degrees. I actually like to have more negative available than I ever intend to use, and I adjust the collective during the descent. This means that I won't have the stick at the bottom of the case; it will be in an intermediate position. Using this technique, I have more negative collective pitch in reserve if I start to overshoot.

In a similar way, try increasing maximum collective pitch until you get blade stall. That usually occurs at about 14 degrees, but it varies with rotor-blade design, true angle of attack, etc. A higher collective-pitch setting would give you more reserve lift available for landing, and that could come in handy in the future. But there's a disadvantage to increasing the pitch range: the collective becomes more sensitive. Helicopters vary, so experiment to get your flying just as you like it.

Aerobatics

An RC helicopter that's properly designed and set up for aerobatics can do virtually anything a fixed-wing plane can do, and much more, with a great deal of precision and grace. This is especially impressive to those who haven't seen a helicopter perform. To see it do a loop and hear the blades slapping against the wind as it pulls out at the bottom is something you won't quickly forget. At first, the sight and sound of the helicopter as it "max" performs, may be a little unnerving to you, but modern helicopters are designed to withstand the stresses involved, and the sound of the blades cutting the air as they change their angle of attack is almost like applause at the end of the maneuver. I think you can tell by now that I'm very fond of aerobatics, and after just a few maneuvers, I'm sure that you will be, too.

Throughout the previous chapters, I've tried to emphasize several important points that you should understand before you set out with a specific objective with your helicopter. First, it's important to understand the basic aerodynamics involved: how the helicopter controls are used, which setup changes may be required to optimize its performance for training and which outside factors (sun, wind, direction of turn, etc.) should be considered. As you progress into the many forms of helicopter aerobatics, however, it becomes more difficult to make precise recom-mendations for your specific helicopter. So much depends on your helicopter's design, its size and its power and radio system. So, as we go through the more advanced maneuvers, be aware that your helicopter may not perform as described, and that you may need to develop different techniques or setup parameters for your helicopter if it's to deliver the performance you want.

By experimenting with changes in the main-rotor and tail-rotor blades, you'll be making some of the most dramatic changes possi-ble to your helicopter. New, lightweight rotor blades are now available to improve your heli-copter's strength and performance. By talking to your local dealer, going to helicopter fly-ins and contests and reading helicopter magazines, you should be able to make an educated deci-sion about which set of blades will meet your needs.

COLLECTIVE PITCH REQUIREMENTS

As you progress, you'll discover an ever-increasing need to match the helicopter's collective pitch to the specific maneuver being per-formed. The more advanced helicopter radios provide more flight modes and pitch-curve refinements to make advanced maneuvering easier and more enjoyable. But even if your radio has a limited capability, you can still follow the discussion and apply what you can to your radio and helicopter combination.

A flight mode is usually acti-vated by a switch on your radio, and it defines the parameters for that particular setting. You may use one flight mode for hovering, another (throttle hold) for auto-rotations and another (idle-up) for aerobatics. Some radios have only two or three flight modes and limited collective-pitch adjust-ments, while more advanced radios have several flight modes and computer adjustments for collective-pitch curves, throttle curves and many other adjust-ments. These radios actually allow you to program them completely for a specific maneuver and to change from one program to another for calm or windy weather. Because of the additional control such advanced radios pro-vide, I recommend that you fly with the best radio you can afford.

When you set up your radio and helicopter for aerobatics, one of the first questions to consider is what you'll use your available flight modes for.

Usually, normal flight mode (with everything else turned off) is used for hovering, throttle-hold is used for autorotations, and additional flight modes such as idle-up are used for aerobatics. Because we've already discussed normal hovering and autorota-tions, let's concentrate on more advanced flight modes, or idle-ups.

If you have only one additional flight mode, your choice is rather limited. That's what you'll use for aerobatics. But if you have several more flight modes, you must

decide which to use with which maneuver. As an example, let's say that you decide on the following:
• Normal flight mode—hovering and normal flying
• Throttle hold—autorotation landings
• Idle-up 1—aerobatics
• Idle-up 2—inverted flying

Now that you've defined what you'd like to do with your radio, there are many techniques for setting it and your helicopter up for the performance you want. And the more advanced your radio, helicopter and the maneuver you want to do, the more you'll need to define your own techniques for setup. First, always set up your helicopter mechanically, and then use the radio adjustments to refine the flight-mode parameters.

Although collective-pitch requirements will depend on the helicopter's rotor-blade design, its engine power and your own flying tastes, the following is an estimate of the collective-pitch requirements for each of the flight modes listed above. Note that these are all initial estimates, and you may, therefore, need to modify them later to improve the helicopter's performance.

Radio setups

Flight mode	Collective pitch	
	Low	High
Normal	-3°	10°
Hold	-5°	14°
Idle-up 1	-3°	10°
Idle-up 2	-10°	10°

The first consideration is the total pitch range, or "window," that you'll need to perform these maneuvers. The lowest pitch is -10 degrees for inverted flying, and the highest pitch is 14

degrees for autorotations; therefore, you need a total pitch window of 24 degrees. Now you must check your helicopter's mechanical collective-pitch limits to see whether it can provide the pitch window you want. To do this, remove the pushrod from the collective-pitch arm, move the pushrod to the high-pitch position, and read the pitch using a pitch gauge. Do the same at the low-pitch position and calculate the window available. Notice that we aren't interested in setting the maximum and minimum collective pitch right now; we're merely determining the available window.

A 24-degree collective-pitch window is quite large, and your helicopter may not have such a large window. If this is the case, the question is, where do you want to reduce the collective-pitch setting to come within your helicopter's available window? Let's say your helicopter is capable only of a 22-degree window. You could reduce the maximum collective pitch on "hold" from 14 degrees to 12 degrees. This would reduce the collective-pitch requirements from -10 degrees for inverted flying to 12 degrees for autos with a 22-degree window.

Next, adjust the radio to provide the pitch window you need. Start with a fresh program, and set all the throws to 100 percent. (Note that some radios may be able to provide more than 100-percent throw.) Then attach the collective-pitch pushrod to the servo so that the full collective-pitch range is reached with full servo movement. This will require you to move the pushrod inwards or outwards on the servo arm or to drill an intermediate hole until you achieve the pitch range.

Now that you have the pitch window you want, you need to adjust the collective pitch for each

flight mode. Starting with the normal flight mode, use the radio collective-pitch adjustments to reduce the low-end pitch to -3 degrees. This is rather easy to do with a pitch gauge on the helicopter set to -3 degrees. In a similar way, adjust the top pitch to 10 degrees. You now have the correct collective-pitch range for the normal flight mode, and you can repeat the procedure for each additional flight mode. (Note: because of the symmetry of inverted flying, many like to have a straight pitch curve from -10 to 10 degrees, with zero degrees at center stick.)

SWASHPLATE

For aerobatic flying, the swashplate must be set up to tilt through its maximum designed range. Move the pushrods on the aileron and elevator servos farther out on the servo arms until you obtain full swashplate movement at full stick throw in all directions. Closely inspect all the linkages between the swashplate and the head to ensure that there's no binding in any extreme position.

POWER REQUIREMENTS

Having the proper collective-pitch setting doesn't do us much good if we don't have the power to keep the rotor blades turning at the correct speed. Aggressive aerobatic maneuvering, which imposes high aerodynamic loads on the helicopter, requires the maximum available engine power. You can increase power by increasing the nitro content of your fuel and/or using a tuned pipe/muffler instead of a regular muffler. Current practical limits of about 30-percent nitro allow a noticeable increase in power without running the engine too lean.

Regardless of which engine/fuel combination you use, it's important to match the engine's

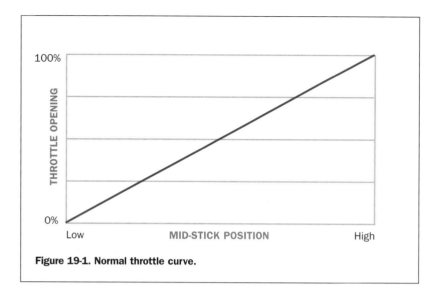

Figure 19-1. Normal throttle curve.

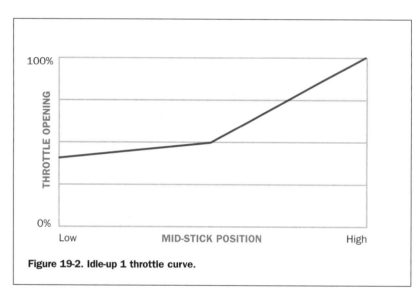

Figure 19-2. Idle-up 1 throttle curve.

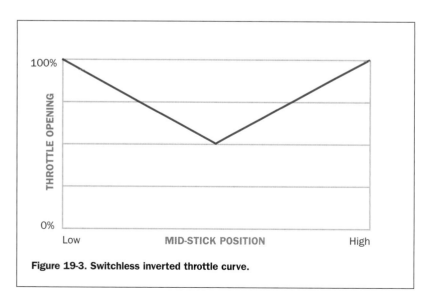

Figure 19-3. Switchless inverted throttle curve.

power output to the requirements of each flight mode. This means that for optimum performance, you must adjust the throttle curve for each of the pitch curves. The normal and throttle-hold "curves" are fairly straightforward. In the normal flight mode, a straight line from the engine cutoff (at low-throttle trim) to full power should work well. In the throttle-hold mode, adjust the throttle to a reliable idle setting. When doing rolls, etc., you will, however, need an increased power setting to maintain high rotor speeds while at low throttle/collective (T/C) stick for idle-up 1. As a starting point, try a low throttle-curve setting of about 40-percent power, as shown in Figure 19-2.

The throttle curve for idle-up 2 (used for inverted flying) poses a unique problem because of the large changes in the helicopter's requirements. Full power is required while at high positive and negative pitch settings, and a lower power is desirable at around the 0 pitch setting where blade drag is at a minimum. This results in the need for a V-shaped throttle curve, as shown in Figure 19-3.

In place of the "V" throttle curve, you could use a governor. This device senses rotor rpm and sends a signal to the throttle servo to maintain the desired rpm. This is certainly a nice option to have, since it will attempt to maintain the desired rpm throughout any maneuver, regardless of pitch setting or loading on the helicopter.

A rev limiter is similar to a governor in that it also senses rpm, but it merely limits the maximum obtainable rpm. This allows you to adjust power requirements with a specific flight-mode throttle curve for a specific maneuver, or series of maneuvers, while still preventing a rotor over-speed at low pitch settings.

TAIL-ROTOR ADJUSTMENTS WITHOUT A HEADING-HOLD GYRO

In the normal flight mode, you should use automatic tail-rotor compensation to adjust the tail rotor when climbing and descending to keep the nose pointing in one direction. But if it's used in idle-up 1 while performing a roll, large variations in yaw will result. It's therefore usual to turn off tail-rotor compensation in anything but the normal flight mode and to instead use rudder offset.

Rudder offset allows you to adjust the tail rotor's neutral position without radio compensation during climbs and descents. The assumption is that idle-up 1 will be used when in fast-forward flight, so the vertical fin on the helicopter will act as a rudder to help keep the nose straight, thereby relieving some of the work required by the tail rotor. Also, the tail rotor itself becomes more effective in fast forward flight (remember translational lift), so it requires less than in the normal hover setting.

To adjust the tail rotor in idle-up 1, fly the helicopter in fast-forward flight and note whether it yaws to one side or the other. Make minor pitch changes until the helicopter is in coordinated straight flight in idle-up 1. You will then have to switch between the normal flight mode and idle-up 1, depending on the performance you want from your helicopter.

Tail-rotor (T/R) compensation for inverted flying (because this isn't normally a fast-forward flight mode) is similar to the "V" throttle-curve setting in that an increase in T/R pitch is needed at both high positive and negative collective-pitch settings with a low T/R pitch at the midrange, or 0 collective-pitch setting. This independent flight mode results in a T/R pitch curve that's similar to that shown in Figure 18-3. Adjust the maximum and minimum portions of the curve to prevent the helicopter from yawing at extreme pitch settings, both upright and inverted. Further refinements to the curve will be needed as you try tumbles and other advanced inverted maneuvers, but that's beyond the scope of this book.

Using a heading-hold gyro greatly simplifies tail-rotor setup and eliminates the need for tail-rotor compensation. This improvement in yaw stability is directly responsible for our having been able to advance helicopter 3D aerobatics over the past few years. You certainly don't need a heading-hold gyro in your helicopter, but I can't think of a better investment for long-term flying enjoyment.

The electronics in a heading-hold gyro allow you to set and forget the helicopter's heading with the gyro making constant adjustments to the tail rotor to keep it in the desired position. This is completely different from a rate gyro, which senses yaw movement and then applies a correcting signal to the tail rotor to stop the movement. A rate gyro, however, makes no attempt to bring the tail rotor back to its original position.

ON WITH THE AEROBATICS

Several years ago, it seemed impossible that a helicopter (full-size or a model) would ever perform a loop. But now, a loop is a common model helicopter maneuver, and even some full-scale helicopters are able to loop. Although the maneuver isn't particularly difficult with the newer RC helicopter designs, your first loop still requires forethought and planning, and it's best done by first working up to a loop by doing a stall turn, a chandelle and an oblique loop.

THE STALL TURN

The stall turn is shown in Figure 19-4 and is used as a warm-up

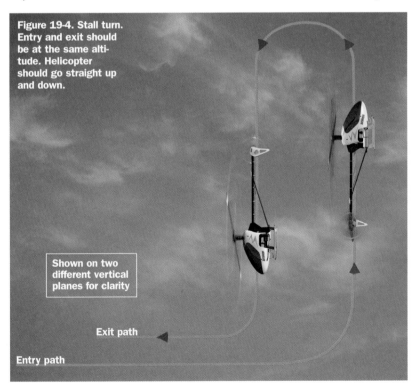

Figure 19-4. Stall turn. Entry and exit should be at the same altitude. Helicopter should go straight up and down.

Shown on two different vertical planes for clarity

Exit path

Entry path

maneuver for the loop because it allows you to enter and recover from a loop while leaving out the middle part. It also allows you to see the model in new and different positions, and it again builds your confidence in your ability to control and recover the helicopter.

For any aerobatic maneuvers, I like to use an exponential control function, if the radio has one. This lets me soften the neutral, but it still allows full swashplate movement when the control stick is moved to extremes. If your radio doesn't have exponential, try increasing the swashplate throw little by little, and fly around to get the feel of the helicopter. If you can, keep increasing the control movement until you can fly with full swashplate throw. If you can't fly with full swashplate movement and comfortably control the helicopter, try using the dual-rate switches to give full throw when you need it for aerobatics, and use a reduced rate for other flying.

Some radios also have a second idle-up function, and this is particularly handy for aerobatics. Adjust the idle-up 1 to keep the rotor speed constant during approaches and landings, and set the idle-up 2 to give nearly full power for aerobatics.

Begin the stall turn rather mildly, as shown in Figure 19-5. The stall turn is usually done with the helicopter climbing in the vertical plane, but to start your practice, let the nose climb only to the 45-degree position, to aid recovery, if needed.

For your first practice maneuver, bring the helicopter in forward flight at a height of 50 feet or so, preferably flying downwind (with the wind), and turn on idle-up 1. After the helicopter has passed you and you're looking at its rear quarter, which is a familiar position, bring its nose up

Figure 19-5. "Mild" stall turn. Decreased pitch attitude makes the stall turn easier.

Figure 19-6. The 540-degree turn is similar to the stall turn, but an additional 360-degree turn is performed at the top of the maneuver.

540° turn

until it is about 45 degrees nose-high. As the helicopter slows almost to a stop, use the tail rotor to move the nose to alter the position into a 45-degree dive. As the helicopter dives and picks up forward speed, continue to add aft cyclic to bring it back to level flight into the wind. I like to fly this maneuver downwind because the helicopter seems to come to a complete stop as the nose is turned, and the recovery is made into the wind, so the vertical fin again keeps the nose straight with minimum tail-rotor control.

Continue to practice this maneuver, taking the nose to a higher and higher attitude each time until the helicopter reaches the vertical plane, as shown in Figure 19-4. As the nose is raised higher, you may also need to reduce the collective as the helicopter reaches the vertical position. Each time you enter and recover the helicopter, evaluate how much aft cyclic it needed and how much was available to make sure that you don't get into a position where you don't have enough control movement to recover.

Another advanced variation on the stall turn is the 540-degree stall turn, as shown in Figure 19-6. The maneuver is flown in the same way as the normal stall turn, but now, the tail rotor is used to swing the nose around one-and-a-half times, or 540 degrees. To perform the maneuver correctly, the helicopter must travel straight up and then turn and travel straight down, recovering to forward flight at the original entry altitude and speed.

THE CHANDELLE

The chandelle is nothing more than a climbing turn using about 45 degrees of bank to change the direction of flight by 180 degrees, as shown in Figure 19-7. I also like to practice this maneuver from the level flight position and traveling downwind so that I complete the maneuver going into the wind because a lot of forward speed is lost during the climb.

Because this is an altitude-gaining maneuver, you can start it from level flight, going downwind, at a rather low altitude of

25 feet or so. Plan to turn in the direction of the main rotor-blade rotation, so that little if any tail-rotor input will be required. To keep the nose steady, you can also leave the gyro in its usual flight setting.

With the helicopter in forward flight going downwind, let it pass your position so that you're again looking at its rear quarter, and start a climbing turn away from you using about 45 degrees of bank and 30 degrees of pitch attitude. If you turn towards yourself, the helicopter will wind up upright and overhead; this not only destroys the beauty of the maneuver, but it also makes the helicopter rather difficult to control. The collective can usually be left at the position required for a rather fast forward flight, but be prepared to add collective if you need it during the climb.

As the helicopter completes its 180-degree turn, it should again be in level flight but now flying into the wind rather slowly. Here again, the vertical fin will keep the nose pointing into the wind with very little tail-rotor control.

THE OBLIQUE LOOP

This isn't actually a "regular" helicopter maneuver, but it's a way to sneak up on a real loop and determine your helicopter's control responsiveness. Notice in Figure 19-8 that the loop is performed off the vertical at an angle you determine. You'll soon notice that if the angle is flat enough, your helicopter will do a horizontal turn.

Make sure that your idle-up is on to give almost full power, and turn off the dual rates, if you use them. To prevent the nose from swinging, leave the gyro sensitivity at that required for normal flight.

Because you don't know how your helicopter will perform during this maneuver, I recommend

Figure 19-7. Chandelle: a high-performance climbing turn using a maximum 60 degrees of bank and ending in level flight.

Figure 19-8. Oblique loop. Performed off the vertical line; if the angle is flattened, a horizontal turn results, rather than a loop.

flight. Notice that you don't have to change the collective and you only coordinate enough with the tail rotor for coordinated flight. The most important part of this maneuver is the second half, or nose-low portion, because this is the first time the helicopter has been placed in this position.

Because the loop was about 45 degrees on its side, it should be a fairly safe maneuver from which to recover, and it will give you the opportunity to evaluate your helicopter's performance when doing a more vertical loop. If your helicopter did fairly well, try the maneuver again, but this time, a little more in the vertical plane—say 30 degrees off vertical rather than the 45 degrees you just tried. Continue in this way until you feel confident when you pull the nose straight up from forward flight, and the helicopter comes right over the top.

When you feel confident doing this rather "dirty" loop that falls off the top, bring coordination of the collective into play as you start the initial climb. Initially, the collective will be set fairly high to produce the fast forward flight,

that you start at a fairly high altitude, say 75 to 100 feet. In this case, altitude is your friend, because it will give you more time to recover if you need it; but don't go too high, or you might lose orientation with the helicopter.

The initial oblique loop will be done without much coordination from the collective because our objective is first to get the helicopter "over the top" and then to recover it to forward flight. This means that the oblique loop will not be round when viewed from the side but will probably look more like Figure 19-9 from the side view.

With the helicopter in rather fast forward flight and going into the wind at a good altitude, start a chandelle as you did before, but now start the maneuver as the helicopter comes abreast of you so that you'll have a good view of the entire maneuver. Also be careful to apply the aft cyclic smoothly so that the helicopter will climb and turn. If you add aft cyclic very abruptly, the helicop-

ter will "pancake" into the wind and come to a virtual standstill. Use about 45 degrees of bank to make the loop oblique to the vertical, but rather than roll out at the top to level flight as you did before, continue to hold in the aft cyclic so that the nose continues to come around back to level

Figure 19-9. When viewed from the side, an oblique loop looks more elliptical than round.

Figure 19-10. The "ideal" roll. Full aileron is applied to roll the helicopter 360 degrees while maintaining a constant altitude.

but start to reduce the collective to "cruise" setting as you apply aft cyclic so that the usual hover collective is reached as the helicopter passes the vertical position. As the helicopter approaches the top of the loop, the collective should be reduced to 0 degrees, or even slightly negative, to elongate the loop into a rounder maneuver. As the nose drops and passes the vertical position, the collective should again be that required for hover and then, a normal recovery to level flight. These collective settings are only guidelines and may not apply to your helicopter, so try various collective settings throughout the maneuver to achieve a round loop with good forward speed.

THE ROLL

Unlike the loop, no maneuvers can be practiced to prepare for the roll. Attempt your first roll with the idea of completing the maneuver. Some things could go wrong in the process, however, and it would obviously be a good idea to be aware of them and to know the corrective action.

The ideal roll should look like the one done by the helicopter shown in Figure 19-10; it maintains level flight and forward speed while completing 360 degrees of roll. To do this, the hel-

icopter usually requires the maximum available right/left swashplate throw. A sensitive aileron setup isn't usually difficult to control in normal flight, but, if needed, the dual-rate function could be switched on to reduce swashplate movement for normal flight and then turned off for the roll. Notice that the elevator sensitivity doesn't have to be adjusted because the elevator requires very little, if any, movement. The only consideration for the elevator is that it should have enough throw to recover the helicopter from any unusual attitude during practice.

Before you attempt a roll, your helicopter should be in very fast forward flight to provide maximum lift to the rotor system and also to keep the vertical fin active, keeping the nose going first. Also, the direction of roll is important and will depend on the direction in which the main rotor is turning. It's always best to turn into the retreating blade (for clockwise rotation, this would be the right side of the rotor disc where the blade is going from its full forward position to its most rearward position) because the lift on a rotor blade is directionally proportional to the speed at which it's passing through the air, and the blade that's advancing into the flight path has the speed of the

rotating blade plus the helicopter's speed as it goes through the air. Notice that the retreating blade also has the velocity of the advancing blade as it's turning, but now, the helicopter's flight speed is subtracted from the blade speed to give it less overall lift than the advancing blade. This is actually very desirable in a roll because the rolling action takes place when the lift on one side of the helicopter is greater than on the other, and you'll further change that lift by using the right/left cyclic control.

For the reasons cited and because the helicopter movement across the sky is slower, I prefer to practice rolls going into the wind. And because you aren't used to your helicopter's roll capabilities, you should attempt the maneuver from a fairly high altitude—at least high enough to recover if the helicopter has to be pulled through the last half of a loop (commonly referred to as a "split-S").

A perfect roll is shown in Figure 19-10, but if any problems develop, the helicopter will lose altitude very quickly while inverted. This likelihood of this can't be completely eliminated, but it can be helped by flying the roll as shown in Figure 19-11. In this roll, the nose is raised slightly to start the helicopter climbing

Figure 19-11. Starting the roll from a slight climb makes the maneuver easier.

away from the ground, and then a full aileron command is given for the roll. As the helicopter rolls onto its back, without any other command but "roll," the nose will fall through level flight, and the maneuver should end in a slight dive. Now, let's go through the entire maneuver and see what can go wrong and how to recover.

With the helicopter in fast forward flight at a high altitude and going into the wind, raise its nose slightly to start a shallow climb. Once it's climbing, reduce the elevator control to that required for level flight, and apply full aileron in the direction of roll. The helicopter should continue to roll, but one or more of the following problems could develop:

• The helicopter's roll rate is too slow. You may notice this before it ever passes 90 degrees of roll, and it will look as if it can't make it around to complete the maneuver. If this happens, abort the maneuver by reversing the aileron command to recover the helicopter to level flight. This absence of roll capability could be caused by

flybar weights damping the effect of the paddles, heavy/thick paddles, heavily weighted blades, reduced aileron throw, or a helicopter design that can't perform the maneuver.

• The helicopter may reduce or completely stop its roll rate in the inverted position. In this situation, it would be best to center the aileron control and recover from the back side of a loop, or split-S, by applying up-elevator.

• The helicopter may continue to roll, but forward flight stops. This could be caused by your holding up-elevator during the roll. If the helicopter continues to roll, let it do so and return to forward flight. Helicopters may go through other gyrations when they stop their forward flight upside-down. In this case, pay more attention to the elevator control to recover the helicopter from the dive, and then recover to forward flight. This is one reason why it's a good idea to master nose-in hovering and flight before you try aerobatics in case the helicopter is facing you during the recovery.

Notice that so far, I haven't mentioned the throttle or collective. Both of these control functions will come into play as you increase your roll proficiency. Begin by setting the idle-up 2 to nearly full power, and if you can separately adjust the collective limit in this idle-up mode, I recommend that you start at a 0-degrees setting. Now, as you roll to the inverted position, you can reduce the collective to the full low position to prevent the helicopter from dropping as it's inverted. The amount of collective required in the inverted position will depend on your particular helicopter design and its entry attitude, so experiment with various negative-collective settings until the helicopter will roll from level flight without losing altitude. As a general rule, faster forward flight at entry will require a more nose-down attitude, so during the roll, you'll need more negative pitch to keep the helicopter at altitude and in forward flight.

INVERTED FLIGHT

Our helicopters have progressed in design to the point at which we can do all the maneuvers that full-scale helicopters can do; in fact, in the case of inverted flying, we've surpassed the "big boys." For crowd appeal, there's nothing like flying inverted, making a low pass and following this with inverted hovering. Like all the other maneuvers, at first, it looks quite difficult, but when looked at logically with the helicopter and radio set up properly, it really isn't very difficult at all.

Before we get into the actual setup and practice, we need to discuss some theory and make a few preparations. Please refer to Figure 19-12, which shows a helicopter in inverted flight.

Some of the basic concepts shown here are:

• The helicopter must be in a nose-low attitude to maintain forward flight.

• The radio hasn't changed the aileron control, and right stick movement still gives the same right/left movement in the helicopter.

• The elevator has been reversed, so aft control-stick movement will lower the nose.

• The tail rotor has also been reversed to give proper movement.

• The collective function has been reversed.

Stick sensitivity in the inverted position is about the same as with the helicopter in normal, upright flight, even though the rotor system seems to be more efficient while inverted. I say it "seems" more efficient because it usually requires less collective pitch to fly/hover while inverted than upright; this is because the helicopter structure is on top of the helicopter, leaving an unrestricted path for the downwash. If your helicopter usually hovers in the 3-degree range while upright, it will probably hover inverted in the -2-degree or -2½-degree range.

One important point to make here is that I'll always discuss blade pitch as if the helicopter were upright on your workbench. This can be a little confusing because when inverted, the rotor blades are actually at a positive pitch in reference to the rest of the world, but in our thinking and setup, with the helicopter upright, it's easier and more consistent to think of the pitch as being negative.

Some of the finer points illustrated in Figure 19-12 are:

• The airfoil design of the main rotor has a lot to do with the helicopter's inverted performance. A fully symmetrical design should give the same performance whether upright or inverted, and a flat-bottom design is severely restricted in its inverted performance and may require excessively negative angles of attack. If you have any questions about the inverted capabilities of your rotor-blade design, ask your dealer or blade manufacturer.

Figure 19-12. Inverted flight. Negative collective pitch is now required to counter the weight and to provide enough thrust for forward flight.

• Most fuel tanks are mounted slightly lower than the engine carburetor for optimum performance during normal flight. But when inverted, the fuel tank is higher than the carburetor and could cause the engine to run slightly richer. This richer engine mixture could cause rotor speed to be reduced to the point at which full power and negative collective won't keep the helicopter in flight. This could happen even when you use muffler pressure to pressurize the fuel tank; a quick solution is to use a pump between the tank and the engine.

The radio equipment—and especially the gyro and large battery pack—are "hung" upside-down. The radio is usually mounted while the helicopter is upright using ties, rubber bands, or double-stick tape to keep it in place. You must obviously take care to ensure that everything will be secure while the helicopter is inverted, or the heavier parts could loosen and become disconnected.

The increased collective range required for inverted flight makes the overall collective response very sensitive compared with what you've been used to. This isn't usually a problem in forward flight, but it will show up while you're hovering because just a little movement on the collective stick will have marked effects on the helicopter.
When you're ready to try inverted flying, wait for a clear day with no more than a light breeze, and fly the helicopter high enough to allow you to recover from any attitude. The helicopter should be in moderate forward flight and pointing into the wind to slow your ground speed. With the idle-up turned on, roll to the inverted position when the helicopter has flown past you and you're looking at its rear quarter.

Also, at first, don't be too concerned with mastering inverted flight, but just practice how to enter and return to normal level flight. When you practice the maneuver for real, stay inverted only for a very few seconds—let's say no more than 5 seconds for the first time. You should just be getting the feel of the helicopter while it's inverted and getting your brain to imagine that it's really right-side up for the controls. As you feel more and more comfortable getting into and out of inverted flight, extend the time spent inverted, but at no time now should you attempt any turns. Your goal now is to get inverted, fly straight and level for a few seconds and then recover to the normal upright position. Keep doing that until you feel really comfortable, and all the shakes have gone.

When you do roll inverted, you may also find that the helicopter is slightly out of elevator trim. More often than not, depending on which helicopter I'm flying, I need a few clicks of down-elevator trim while inverted. I do this just before starting the maneuver because if you can avoid it, you shouldn't adjust the trims while flying inverted.

As you feel increasingly comfortable in inverted flight, you can't just keep going straight, or the helicopter will fly out of sight, so you must eventually turn it. The thing to remember here is that the rotor system is turning in the opposite direction to when the helicopter was upright. This means that the helicopter will also turn better in the opposite direction than when it was upright. So most helicopters that have a clockwise rotation will turn more easily to the left than to the right while inverted and, therefore, all turns should be to the left. That isn't to say the helicopter won't turn to the right; it's just that more tail-rotor coordination will be required.

Also be careful during the turns to keep the bank angle very shallow. This will help to reduce the amount of elevator required in the turns, and it will also enable you to stay better oriented with the helicopter.

If orientation with the helicopter becomes a problem, a solution may be found in the main blades. A dark-colored blade is usually hard to see in flight and may not be visible at all. If your rotor blades are dark, put 3-inch strips of white blade-covering material near each tip and again 3 inches farther down the blade. Now, when the blades are turning, the white will show up as two concentric circles, and these will keep you oriented with the rotor's plane.

As you progress with your inverted flying, you'll find it rather easy to reduce collective for a descent and then transition into a hover. With all that mass above the rotor plane, it's amazing how the helicopter is completely stable while inverted, even while hovering. And once you've done that, it's time for inverted hovering, pirouettes and inverted autos. That should add a little excitement to your life!

After practicing the inverted position for an extended time, be especially careful when you return to upright: it may no longer be the "normal" position for you because you've been trying very hard to reverse many of the controls. This means that you may accidentally make an inverted control response to an upright helicopter movement. This is to be expected at first, but soon, flipping from upright to inverted will be just another maneuver.

3D FLYING

When you've mastered the basics, the sky's the limit for flips, tumbles, backward flying, backward loops and 3D maneuvers.

All these maneuvers require a combination of the following:

Equipment and setup: 3D flying requires optimum performance from all your equipment—helicopter, radio, engine, etc. High-quality equipment designed for the most severe stress is a must-have to handle the high aerodynamic forces involved.

No helicopter or radio can fly optimum 3D maneuvers "out of the box." It takes time and trial and error to find the best combination of pitch curves, idle-up, mixing programs, etc., to make your helicopter feel just right for you. And what feels right to you may not be right for someone else. Certainly, get all the information you can from fellow fliers, but use that with your own flying style to set up your equipment.

Using the wind: As a rule, maneuvers that move the helicopter in the vertical are best flown into the wind. This is because the main rotor acts like a wing, and the oncoming wind will provide extra lift. In a similar way, maneuvers that maintain a constant altitude and move in the horizontal are best performed while flying downwind. This will help to mask any minor changes in altitude during the maneuver.

Understanding forces on the helicopter:
• Momentum. I like to think of this as placing a small force on the helicopter for a short time to get it moving in the direction I want. As an example of momentum, imagine having a tennis ball in the palm of your hand, then you loft it up to about a foot, and then catch it as it falls. This process takes just over a second, and the ball went 1 foot up and one foot down. For many helicopter maneuvers, especially those moving downwind, this 1-foot difference in altitude would not be noticed by anyone watching, including the pilot. It does, however, get the helicopter moving in the vertical for a second or so, and this gives us enough time to do at least part of the maneuver.

• Lift. As you know, lift is produced by the main rotor system, and it can be positive, negative, or neutral. All three possibilities become important as we go through a typical 3D maneuver.

As a rule, we would like to have positive lift when the helicopter is in the normal upright position, neutral lift when the rotor system passes through the vertical position and negative lift as the rotor system is inverted.

FINAL THOUGHTS

When I work on any project, I always think I can accomplish more before I call it complete, and that's how I feel about this book. There's always more equipment to be tried and written about—explained using different words and used with different techniques. But the book has to be printed, or I could have the best book in the world, but it would be confined to my computer where no one else could read it.

I'd appreciate your comments and thoughts on the book; you can contact me through the publisher. Did you learn what you wanted to know? Do you know additional techniques that you think are better? Does the book cover enough material?

I certainly couldn't have written this without the help of the following manufacturers and distributors. I know they would appreciate your asking for their products.

22nd Century Aero Products
Ace Hobby Distributors
Airtronics
AstroFlight
Century Helicopter Products
Champion Model Products
Curtis Youngblood Inc.
Dave Brown Products
Dobyns Enterprises
Du-Bro
ElectroDynamics
Equalizer
FMA Direct
Futaba Corp. of America
Great Planes Model Distributors
Hitec RCD Inc
Hobby People
Hobbytech
Horizon Hobby Inc.
Ikarus
JPB Custom Helicopter Accessories
LDM Industries Inc.
Lite Machines
Miniature Aircraft
Model Avionics
Model Rectifier Corp.
Petal Mfg.
Precision Model Products
Solder-it Co.
SR Batteries Inc.
Thunder Tiger
V-Blades
Wahoo Intl.
West Mountain Radio
Wildcat Fuels

22nd Century Aero Products (805) 943-5394.
A&A Engineering (714) 952-2114; a-aengineering.com.
Ace Hobby Distributors (949) 833-0088; acehobby.com.
Aces of Iron Productions Inc.; acesofiron.com.
Advanced Scale Models; dist. by Global Hobby.
Aero-Model Inc. (480) 963-5565; aero-model.com.
Aerospace Composite Products; acp-composites.com.
Aeroworks (303) 366-4205; aero-works.net.
Air Craft Inc.; aircraft-world.com.
Air Dynamics (718) 396-4765; airdyn.com.
AirBorne Models (925) 371-0922; airborne-models.com.
Airfoil Aviation Inc. (217) 938-4473; airfoilaviation.com.
Airplane Factory Inc. (800) 264-7840.
Airtronics dist. by Global Hobby.
Alfa Models; dist. by Hobby Lobby.
Align; dist. by Assurance RC (562) 926-5357; alignrcusa.com.
America's Hobby Center; ahc1931.com.
Amondo Tech (408) 747-1123; amondotech.com.
Aon Electric (310) 470-5188; aonelectric.com.
Apache; dist. by BP Hobbies & PFM Dist.
APC Props; dist. by Landing Products; apcprop.com.
Apex; dist. by Magma Intl.
Apogee batteries; dist. by PFM Distribution and Prop Shop Hobbies.
AstroFlight Inc. (310) 821-6242; astroflight.com.
Atec Models (863) 709-8088; atecmodels.com.
Autogyro Co. of Arizona; autogyro-rc.com.
Axi; dist. by Hobby Lobby and Northeast Sailplane.
Balsa Products; see BP Hobbies.
Batteries America (608) 831-3443; batteriesamerica.com.
Berg; dist. by Castle Creations.
Bergen Machine & Tool (616) 445-2060.
Bisson Custom Mufflers (705) 389-1156; bissonmufflers.com.
Blue Arrow; ltair.com.
Blue Bird; dist. by BP Hobbies.
Bluejay Airplane Kits (308) 276-2322; bridiairplanes.com.
BME Engines (604) 638-3119; bmeengine.com.
Bob Banka's Scale Aircraft Documentation (714) 979-8058; bobsairdoc.com.
Bob Selman Designs (417) 358-9521; bsdmicrorc.com.
Bob Smith Industries (805) 466-1717; bsiadhesives.com.
Bob Violett Models (BVM) (407) 327-6333; bvmjets.com.
Boca Bearing Co. (561) 998-0004; bocabearings.com.
BP Hobbies [formerly Balsa Products] (732) 287-3933; bphobbies.com.
Bruckner Hobbies (800) 288-8185; brucknerhobbies.com.
Brushless Motors Inc. (BMI) (386) 985-0288; brushless-motor.com.
Byron Originals (712) 364-3165; byronfuels.com.
C.F. Lee Mfg. Co., 10112 Woodward Ave., Sunland, CA 91040.
Cactus Aviation (520) 721-0087; cactusaviation.com.
CAF96th Squadron; caf96th.com.
Cajun R/C Specialties (337) 269-5177.
Cal-Grafx; cal-grafx.com.
CAModel USA (786) 999-6253; camodel.com.ar.
Carbon Extreme; carbonxtreme.com.
Carden Aircraft (828) 697-7177.
Carl Goldberg Products Ltd. (678) 450-0085; carlgoldbergproducts.com.
Castle Creations (785) 883-4519; castlecreations.com.

Cedar Hobbies (832) 202-7343; cedarhobbies.com.
Century Helicopter Products (800) 686-8588; centuryheli.com.
Century Jet Models (502) 266-9234; centuryjet.com.
Cermark (562) 906-0808; cermark.com.
Champion Model Products (909) 599-3348.
Charger RC; chargerrc.com.
Chase-Durer (800) 544-4365; chase-durer.com.
CheapBatteryPacks.com (503) 356-5567.
Chief Aircraft Inc. (877) 219-4489; chiefaircraft.com.
Cirrus; dist. by Global Hobby Dist.
Cleveland Model & Supply Co. (317) 257-7878.
Communications Specialists Inc. (800) 854-0547; com-spec.com.
Composite ARF Co. Ltd.; composite-arf.com.
Cool Power; dist. by Morgan Fuels.
Coverite; dist. by Great Planes.
Cox Models; coxmodels.com.
Crusader Toys crusadertoys.com.
CSM; rcmodels.org/csm.
C-Tronics (201)818-4289; c-tronicsinc.com
Curtis Youngblood Inc.; curtisyoungblood.com.
D&L Designs (520) 887-0771.
Dave Brown Products (513) 738-1576; dbproducts.com.
Dave Patrick Models (815) 457-3128; davepatrickmodels.com.
Davis Model Products (203) 877-1670.
Deans Connectors; W.S. Deans Co. (714) 828-6494; wsdeans.com.
Debece Co. (615) 238-4884; debece.net.
Desert Aircraft (520) 722-0607; desertaircraft.com.
Diversity Model Aircraft (858) 693-8188.
Dobyns Enterprises; distributed by Horizon Hobby.
Doppeldecker Corp. (800) 777-2090; 2decker.com.
Double M Electronics (301) 805-9361.
Dremel Tool (800) 437-3635; dremel.com.
Dry-Set Model Markings (817) 741-0335.
Du-Bro Products (800) 848-9411; dubro.com.
Dumas (800) 458-2828.
Duralite Batteries (877) 744-3685; duralitebatteries.com.
DWE (Dynamic Web Enterprises/Dynamics Unlimited (727) 559-0539; slowfly.com.
Eagle Tree Systems (888) 432-4744; eagletreesystems.com.
EaglePicher Kokam Ltd.; dist. by FMA Direct.
Eddie A. Aircraft Original Scale Classics (201) 337-5075.
EF Helicopters; dist. by Global Hobby.
E-flite; dist. by Horizon Hobby Inc.
Electric Jet Factory (520) 579-5609; ejf.com.
ElectriFly; dist. by Great Planes.
ElectroDynamics (734) 422-5420.
Empire Hobby (480) 982-0909; empirerc.com.
Enya; dist. by MRC.
Equalizer; (800) 334-1334; equalizer.com.
Evergreen Scale Models Inc. (425) 402-4918; evergreenscalemodels.com.
Evolution engines; dist. by Horizon Hobby Inc.
Experimental Aircraft Models (800) 297-1707.
F&M Enterprises (817) 279-8045; stits.com.
Falcon Trading Co. (800) 591-2896; falcon-trading.com.
Feigao; feigao.com.

FHS Supply & Mfg.; members.aol.com/FHSoil.
Fiberglass Specialties (810) 677-0213.
Flight Line Toys (417) 883-2510.
Flying Styro; dist. by Hobby Lobby.
FlyZone; dist. by Great Planes.
FMA Direct (800) 343-2934; fmadirect.com.
Fox Mfg. (479) 646-1656; foxmanufacturing.com.
Fox Models (319) 322-1244.
FPF Inc. (877) FLY-FOAM; fpf-inc.com.
Futaba; dist. by Great Planes; futaba-rc.com.
G and P Sales (707) 965-1216.
Georgia Aircraft Modelers Assoc. (478) 328-2689; gama.rcclubs.com.
Glenn Torrance Models (919) 643-1001; gtmodels.
Global Hobby Distributors (714) 963-0329; globalhobby.com.
Graupner; dist. by Hobby Lobby Intl.
Great Northern Models (905) 320-7979.
Great Planes Model Distributors (217) 398-6300; (800) 682-8948; greatplanes.com.
Grich RC Inc. (732) 873-1519; grichrc.com.
GWS USA (909) 594-4979; gwsus.com.
Hacker Brushless Motors (937) 256-7727; hackerbrushless.com.
Hangar 9; dist. by Horizon Hobby.
Hayes Products (714) 554-0531.
HeliHobby; helihobby.com.
Heli-Max; dist. by Great Planes.
Helitronix helitronix.com.
Himax; dist. by MPI.
Hirobo; dist. by MRC.
Hitec RCD Inc. (858) 748-6948; hitecrcd.com.
Hobbico; dist. by Great Planes; hobbico.com.
Hobbies & Helis Intl. (610) 282-4811.
Hobby Group Inc. (562) 240-2134; nwhobbyexpo.com.
Hobby Lobby Intl. (615) 373-1444; hobby-lobby.com.
Hobby People; dist. by Global Hobby (800) 854-8471; hobbypeople.net.
Hobbytech hobbytech-models.com.
HobbyZone; dist. by Horizon; hobbyzonesports.com.
Horizon Hobby Inc. (800) 338-4639; horizonhobby.com.
Hurricane Flight Systems (813) 996-6997; flyhurricane.com.
Hydrimax by Hobbico; dist. by Great Planes.
ICARE Sailplanes (450) 449-9094; icare-rc.com.
Ikarus USA (239) 690-0003; ikarus.net.
Innovative Home Products (866) 607-8736; innovativehomeproducts.com.
Integy; integy.com.
Internet-RC (602) 347-1600; Internet-RC.com.
J&Z Products (310) 539-2313.
J'tec (805) 487-0355; jtecrc.com.
Jet Hangar Hobbies (562) 467-0260.
Jeti; dist. by Hobby Lobby Intl.
JMP; dist. by Bob Selman.
JPB Accessories (810) 444-4558; pcbinkley@verizon.net.
JR Heli Division; dist. by Horizon Hobby.
JR Sport; dist. by Horizon Hobby Inc.
JR; dist. by Horizon Hobby Inc.
K&B Model Products (626) 359-9527; modelengine.com.
K&S Engineering (773) 586-8503; ksmetals.com.
Kangke USA (877) 203-2377; kangkeusa.com.

Kavan; dist. by Sig.
Kinetic Motor Systems; dist. by Global.
Kokam—see EaglePicher Kokam.
Kondor Model Products (888) 968-7251; kmp.ca.
Kontronik; dist. by Great Planes.
Kress Technologies Inc. (845) 336-8149; kressjets.com.
Kyosho Corp. of America (800) 716-4518; kyoshoamerica.com.
Landing Products (530) 661-0399.
Lanier RC (770) 532-6401; lanierrc.com.
LDM Industries Inc. (813) 991-4277.
Litefly RC; liteflyrc.com.
Lite Machines (765) 463-0959; litemachines.com.
Loctite (216) 475-3600; loctiteproducts.com.
Macs Products (916) 456-6932; macspro.com.
Magma Intl. (905) 305-9753; magmarcc.com.
Magnum; dist. by Global Hobby.
Maiden Model Products (612) 730-7151.
Master Airscrew; dist. by Windsor Propeller Co.
Maxx by Lumicorp; maxxlights.com.
Maxx Products Intl. (MPI) (800) 416-6299; maxxprod.com.
Medusa Research Inc. (508) 675-0200; medusaproducts.com.
Mega Motor USA (888) 800-3663; megamotorsusa.com.
Megatech Intl. (201) 662-2800; megatech.com.
Mejzlik; dist. by Desert Aircraft.
Menz propellers; dist. by Desert Aircraft.
Micro Fasteners (908) 806-4050.
Midwest Products (800) 348-3497.
Miller R/C Products (707) 833-5905.
Miniature Aircraft USA (404) 292-4267.
Model Avionics; modelavionics.com.
Model Machining Service (949) 631-2982; innerdemon.com.
Model Master; modelmaster.com.uk.
Model Tech; dist. by Hobby People.
MonoKote; dist. by Great Planes.
Morgan Fuel (800) 633-7556; morganfuel.com.
Mosquitobite Planes (613) 256-0008; mosquitobiteplanes.com.
MP Jet; dist. by Hobby Lobby; mpjet.com.
MPI (800) 416-6299; maxxprod.com.
MRC (732) 225-2100; modelrec.com.
MS Composit (650) 592-8592; mscomposit-usa.com.
MTA Hobbies (310) 533-6868; mtahobbies.com.
Multiplex; dist. by Hitec RCD.
Nick Ziroli Plans (516) 467-4765; ziroliplans.com.
Nitro Models Inc.; nitroplanes.com.
Northeast Sailplane Products (802) 655-7700; nesail.com.
Northeast Screen Graphics (800) 557-5617; majordecals.com.
O.S. Engines; dist. by Great Planes.
Oracover; dist. by Hobby Lobby.
Pacer Technology (800) 538-3091; pacertechnology.com.
Park Pilots; dist. by Kondor Model Products.
Parkflyers.com (732) 363-6181.
ParkZone; dist. by Horizon Hobby Inc.
Paul K. Guillow Inc. (781) 245-5255; guillow.com.
Peck-Polymers (619) 448-1818; peck-polymers.com.
Pegae Model Products (216) 486-5460.
Performance Devices Inc.; (209) 588-0848; performancedevices.com.

Performance R/C (504) 832-2028.

Petal Mfg. (908) 766-7095; petalrc.com.

PFM Distribution (618) 222-2765; pfmdistribution.com.

Phase 3; dist. by Global Hobby.

Plantraco (306) 955-1836; plantraco.com.

Plastruct Inc. (626) 912-7016; plastruct.com.

Polk's Hobby; polkshobby.com.

Polyquest; dist. by Hobby Lobby.

PowerMaster Hobby Products Inc. (512) 285-9595; powermasterfuels.com.

Precision Model Products precisionmodelproducts.com.

Prop Shop Hobbies (586) 757-7160; prop-shop.com.

Propwash Video (800) 355-7333; propwashvideo.com.

Quantum Models (877) 738-9270; qyantummodels.com.

Quique's Aircraft Co.; somenzini.com.

R/C Direct (858) 277-4531; rc-direct.com.

R/C Showcase (301) 374-2197; rcshowcase.com.

Radical RC (937) 237-7889; radicalrc.com.

RAm Radio Controlled Services (847) 740-8726; ramrcandramtrack.com.

RC Showcase (301) 374-2197; rcshowcase.com.

RC Superstore; rcsuperstore.com.

RCAT Systems (408) 292-9794; rcatsystems.com.

RCGuys.com; (519) 756-1110.

RCV Engines Ltd.; dist. by Wildcat Fuels.

Revolution Engines; dist. by Kangke.

Richmond RC Supply (877) 727-2329; richmondrc.com.

Rimfire; dist. by Great Planes.

Ripmax; dist. by Global.

Robart Mfg. (630) 584-7616; robart.com.

RTL Fasteners (800) 239-6010; rtlfasteners.com.

Saito; dist. by Horizon.

Scanlogic (614) 338-1237.

Seagull Models; dist. by Horizon.

Sherline Products Inc. (800) 541-0735; sherline.com.

Sig Mfg. Co. Inc. (800) 247-5008; sigmfg.com.

Simprop; dist. by Hobby Lobby.

SKS Video Productions (800) 988-6488; sksvideo.com.

Sky & Technology (310) 527-0002; sky-technology.net.

Sky Hooks & Rigging (905) 257-2101; microrc.com.

Skyshark R/C Corp. (866) 854-6100; skysharkrc.com.

Slimline Mfg. (480) 967-5053; slimlineproducts.com.

Smiley Antenna (619) 579-8916.

SoarSoft Software (810) 225-1165.

Solder-It Co. (800) 897-8989; solder-it.com.

Sonic-Tronics (215) 635-6520; sonictronics.com.

Spektrum; dist. by Horizon Hobby.

SR Batteries Inc. (631) 286-0079; srbatteries.com.

Sullivan Products (410) 732-3500; sullivanproducts.com.

T&D Plan Sales; classicairplanemodels.com.

Tanic; dist. by R/C Toys; tanicpacks.com.

Team Orion; (714) 694-2812; team-orion.com.

Tekoa: The Center of Design (909) 763-0464.

Testor Corp. (815) 962-6654; testors.com.

The World Models Mfg. Co. Ltd.; dist. in the USA by AirBorne Models; theworldmodels.com.

Thunder Power Batteries; dist. by Hobby Lobby and Northeast Sailplane Products; thunderpower-batteries.com.

Thunder Tiger; dist. by Ace Hobby.

Top Flite; dist. by Great Planes; top-flite.com.

Tower Hobbies (800) 637-4989; towerhobbies.com.

Trick R/C (310) 301-1614; zagi.com.

Tru-Turn Precision Model Products; dist. by Romco Mfg.; tru-turn.com.

U.S. Engines Products; dist. by Great Planes.

UltraCote; dist. by Horizon Hobby.

Ultrafly; dist. by MRC.

Vanguard Vancouver; pacifier.com/~vvancou.

Varsane Products (619) 591-4228.

V-Blades; vblades.com.

Vencon Technologies Inc. (416) 226-2628; vencon.com.

Venom Air Corps (208) 762-0620; venom-aircorps.com.

Wahoo Intl.; solarez.com.

WattAge; dist. by Global Hobby.

WeMoTec; wemotec.com.

West Mountain Radio (203) 853-8080; westmountainradio.com.

Weston USA (508) 520-1170; westonusa.com.

Wildcat Fuels (859) 885-5619; wildcatfuels.com.

Williams Bros.; williamsbrothersmodelproducts.com.

Windsor Propeller Co. (916) 631-8385.

Wing Mfg. (269) 665-9630; wingmfg.com.

WRAM Inc.; wram.org.

Yellow Aircraft Intl. (781) 674-9898; yellowaircraft.com.

Zap (800) 538-3091; zapglue.com.

Zenoah; dist. by Horizon Hobby.

Zinger; dist. by J&Z Products; zingerpropeller.com.

Zooms Heli; zoomsheli.com.

Zurich Intl. (916) 691-6467; zurichsunglasses.com.